Enter the River

Enter the River

Healing Steps from White Privilege Toward Racial Reconciliation

Jody Miller Shearer

Foreword by Michael Banks

HERALD PRESS
Scottdale, Pennsylvania
Waterloo, Ontario

Library of Congress Cataloging-in-Publication Data
Shearer, Jody Miller, 1965-
    Enter the river : healing steps from white privilege toward racial
reconciliation / Jody Miller Shearer.
        p. cm.
    Includes bibliographical references and index.
    ISBN 0-8361-3660-8 (alk. paper)
    1. Racism. 2. Race relations—Religious aspects—Mennonites.
I. Title.
HT1521.S435   1994
305.8—dc20   93-40702
                                                               CIP

The paper used in this publication is recycled and meets the minimum
requirements of American National Standard for Information
Sciences—Permanence of Paper for Printed Library Materials, ANSI
Z39.48-1984.

ENTER THE RIVER
Copyright © 1994 by Herald Press, Scottdale, Pa. 15683
    Published simultaneously in Canada by Herald Press,
    Waterloo, Ont. N2L 6H7. All rights reserved
Library of Congress Catalog Number: 93-40702
International Standard Book Number: 0-8361-3660-8
Printed in the United States of America
Book and cover design by Gwen M. Stamm
Cover photo by Crystal Watts

2 3 4 5 6 7 8 9 10 00 99 98 97 96

*To Cheryl Miller Shearer,
who believed that I could.*

Contents

Foreword

ENTER THE RIVER is both an invitation and a challenge. The book engages readers regardless of which bank of the ethnic river they may be standing on. Through poignant stories and lucid insights, a personal call to a faithful ministry of reconciliation emerges.

The practical biblical discernment that accompanies strategies for change provides guidance to navigate the subtle currents of covert racism that pollute our beliefs, values, and attitudes. The book encouraged me with its prophetic edge—an edge aimed at dismantling the false assumptions reinforced by institutional racism and its cultural handmaidens.

Written by an Anglo-American to Anglo-Americans, *Enter the River* carries the clear perspective and deep compassion of one who has awakened to the unjust privileges accorded whites in North America and calls others to awaken as well.

Although this work aims to challenge the mind-set of those accustomed (whether consciously or not) to white privilege, it beckons all to the healing process. This is because the impact of such an erroneous point of view affects everyone at some level.

Through entering the currents of this book, I further processed both ways the system of white privilege deepens the harmful antagonism between races and ways the gospel offers hope of transformation. Jody Miller Shearer calls the body of Christ to press on toward the truth of the kingdom of God. The flow of the healing river draws all toward participation in the most precious and passionate personal ministry—expressing the reconciling love of Christ.

> —*Michael Banks, pastor, Burnside Mennonite Church;*
> *assistant bishop and area strategist for Lancaster*
> *(Mennonite) Conference churches in New York City*
> *New York, New York*

Preface and Acknowledgments

I LOVE a good story. Whether reading *Where the Wild Things Are* to my children before bedtime, immersing myself in a science fiction novel, or listening to a retelling of the story of Joseph and the coat of many colors, I relish the experience of entering into another world. Stories pull me in, turn me around, and let me see my life from a new perspective.

Jesus knew the power of stories. He told hundreds of them in his lifetime. The Scriptures bear witness to the best of them—the prodigal son, the good Samaritan, the wise and foolish virgins, and many more. The mere mention of these names evokes strong images for all who have heard these parables.

In this book I will share many stories. Much of the time, the characters and plot come from my life. In particular I will tell of how I have come to struggle with my own racism and the racism I encounter in the church and society around me. Sometimes those stories are painful to recall; sometimes they are joyous. I include both kinds because in the telling of a story I find healing.

Scripture stories figure prominently as well. The story found in 2 Kings 5 of Naaman, Elisha, the Israeli slave girl, and the river Jordan will receive much attention. The rest of the stories come from individuals and groups across the church who are also struggling to dismantle racism. These stories carry pain and joy in addition to humor, strength, and courage. They are remarkable not because they tell of exceptional people doing extraordinary things but because they tell of ordinary people doing faithful things.

In the course of telling those stories, we'll look at power, history, relationships, white privilege, the role of structures, and cultural assumptions that maintain religious practice.

Before writing more of stories, let me introduce myself.

A prelude to my story

When I start a book, one of the first things I do is turn to the back flap to read about the author. I want to know about the person who has crafted the world I am about to enter. Usually the dust jacket doesn't carry enough information to satisfy me.

So, assuming that most readers want to know more about the author than what appears on the dust jacket, here are a few bits of information about me. Consider it a prelude to my story.

I'm a white male. My whiteness has never been a matter of dispute—however many junk mail computers, conference lists, and school rosters have placed me in the female column (which caused no small trauma in my younger days).

I love to read. Science fiction and fantasy capture my imagination as no other genre can. I used to say books were my best friends. Having outgrown the more intense edge of my introversion, I can't say that anymore.

In December of 1986, I entered into a marriage covenant with Cheryl Miller. She is my best friend and the mother of my two children, Dylan Moses and Zachary John. Living with Cheryl has helped me to be a little less obsessive about bedmaking, dishwashing, and floor-sweeping. I've even learned to do things spontaneously. During our courtship, I considered it spontaneous if we waited until Monday to decide on Friday's activities.

I am committed to the believer's church. Anabaptism runs through my veins and pumps through my arteries. One of the things I enjoyed about living in New Orleans was that so few people knew about the Mennonites, that particular slice of Anabaptism I call my own. I became adept at explaining our theological peculiarities to Catholics, Methodists, Baptists, and even an occasional Mormon.

Words—their sound, structure, and symbolism—fascinate me. During college I highlighted every new word I looked up in the dictionary as if to claim it as my own. Putting words together is my work. I can't say I love writing, but I love to have written.

I've been told I'm an overachiever. I'll accept that along with some other weaknesses: pastries enter my mouth too easily, electronics tempt me to buy gadgetry I don't need, meeting deadlines and goals carries greater priority for me than spending time with people.

Friendships come slowly for me, but once I find one, it usually lasts a long time. That has meant I've struggled with loneliness on and off through my life. It has also meant I cherish the friends that I have.

The river

By the time you are finished with this book I hope you will have entered into some new stories. But I also hope you will have found resources for evaluating the effects of racism in government, the media, churches, schools, and individual relationships.

Most of all, I hope this book will move you toward healing. Throughout the book I use the metaphor of river because moving water figures so prominently in the story of our world and our faith. Cities spring up next to rivers. Rivers provide easy transport. The children of Israel crossed the Jordan River into a promised land. Jesus was baptized in a river.

In a poetic sense, each story in this book is a stream, each stream leads to the river, and the river is a source of healing. We live in a world afflicted with racism. The affliction leaves us wounded. The river runs over our wounds, enters their depth, cleans them, and leads us on to more healing.

Which river is this? It is the Mississippi and the Jordan. It is the power of love and the necessity of redemption. It is our present, past, and future. It flows through the heart of our nation and the soul of our belief. The river is the hope of racial reconciliation.

Acknowledgments

The following people served on a reference committee for this book: Mark Chupp, Dorothy Friesen, Samuel Lopez, Stan Maclin, Olivette McGhee, Linda Gehman Peachey, Brenda Quant, Loretta Whalen. They read and responded to each chapter with consistently insightful suggestions. Thanks to each for your patience and perseverance in this long process.

Mennonite Central Committee (MCC) provided me with the time and financial support to make the writing of this book a possibility. Titus and Linda Peachey, co-coordinators of MCC U.S. peace and justice ministries, organized the January 1992 meeting during which the idea for this book was originally proposed by Charmayne Denlinger Brubaker of MCC Information Services.

At the same meeting, Lindsey Robinson, associate director for church planter training and resourcing at Eastern Mennonite Board of Missions and Charities, made several comments that planted the seed for the title of the book and the imagery of healing river.

The People's Institute for Survival and Beyond provided me with my first introduction to an analysis of racism and white privilege. Their staff people have continued to challenge and push me to a deeper understanding of the dynamics of racism. Special thanks to David Billings, Ron Chisom, Diana Dunn, and Barbara Major.

Thanks to the staff of Loyola University's Twomey Center for Peace Through Justice for access to computers and printers and many conversations on the topic of racism. Jean Brown, Jeff Gingerich, Richard McCarthy, and Ted Quant deserve special recognition.

In addition to believing that I could, Cheryl Miller Shearer walked with me through the setbacks and disappointments along the way. She also provided steady critique and suggestions as I moved from draft to draft. All this while providing primary care for our two sons, Dylan and Zachary, who get mentioned here just because they're so much fun to be around.

And many thanks to these readers, encouragers, challengers, and friends: Wilma Bailey, Annette Bergen, Tom Eagan, Omar Eby, Berry Friesen, Gloria Firman, Margery Freeman, Nancy Heisey, Rebecca Kreider, Brent Landers, Joanne Lingle, Karen Myers, Harold Nussbaum, Mary Riley, Vel and John Shearer, Carolyn and Dave Shrock-Shenk, Jim Stutzman, Roxene Thiessen, Ron Tinsley, Amy Weaver.

My last acknowledgment is to clearly state that it is a white privilege to be able to write this book on white privilege. The time, financial support, and publishing access given to me spring from systems I have easy access to as a white person. This is not to say a person of color could not have written this book. It just goes to show that white privilege is far more pervasive than most white people are aware. May this book be one way to increase our awareness as we step toward the healing river.

—*Jody Miller Shearer*
Lancaster, Pennsylvania

Enter the River

1

Why Be Concerned About Racism?

W HEN MOST OF US think of racism, we think of the type of story told by Los Angeles Mennonite minister William Irvin.

William attended college at a small school in Dover, Delaware, twelve miles below the Mason-Dixon line. The year was 1959. One weekend evening, William and two of his friends were walking back to campus from town. They came to a restaurant. William and a friend were hungry and decided to get a hamburger. William's other friend said, "You don't want to go in there."

"Why not? We're not scared," they replied.

So William and his friend ordered a hamburger. The restaurant proprietor responded, "Yeah, I'll get you something." He walked into a back room and returned with a shotgun he proceeded to point at them.

"We just walked out," William said, "We laughed, but it wasn't really funny. This guy was going to blow us away just because of our skin color."

We know immediately that the overt racism shown to William and his friend is evil and wrong. White supremacists, members of the KKK, and others who support an Aryan agenda embody this sort of hateful racism in the contemporary scene.

Not limited to the deep South, these incidents of overt racism continue to take place throughout North America. During the 1980s, documented cases of "hate crimes" occurred in forty states and the District of Columbia.[1] Two hundred and thirty organized hate groups have been identified by the Southern Poverty Law Center's Klanwatch Project in Montgomery, Alabama.[2] From New Orleans to New Brunswick, and from L.A to D.C., overt racism rears its ugly head.

Few if any hate group members profess Anabaptist belief. Anabaptists do not fill the ranks of the Ku Klux Klan or other less well-known—but equally dangerous—groups like the Christian Identity Movement. As William Irvin says, "There's still lots of racism in this country, but it has no place in the church. God is the one who made us all different. Just look at Psalm 139:14 'I am fearfully and wonderfully made.' "

So why write a book about racism for members of Anabaptist churches? First of all, God calls us to be part of a caring response to the rise of overt racism in North America. That call appears time and again throughout Scripture. We'll look at many such calls throughout this book, but one of the clearest calls is put forth by the apostle Paul in 2 Corinthians.

> So if anyone is in Christ, there is a new creation: everything old has passed away; see, everything has become new! All this is from God, who reconciled us to himself through Christ, and has given us the ministry of reconciliation. . . .
> (2 Cor. 5:17-18)

To engage in that ministry of reconciliation, we need to understand the dynamics of racism in North America. Even if we do not practice overt racism, we need to be aware of our role in the quagmire of race. From the earliest days of slavery through the present, race has divided North Americans.

As a white person, I am best prepared to write about racism for white audiences. People of color may also find the stories and discussion in this book helpful, but I will write primarily to white members of Anabaptist churches.

And I will write about racism. But I will write more about subtle than overt racism. As we will discuss later, the difference between subtle and overt racism is one not only of content but also of form. Whereas overt racism is made up of raw hate, misplaced pride, and deep fear, subtle racism uses basic assumptions, unexamined systems, and simple prejudice. Whereas overt racism takes the form of physical abuse, verbal harassment, and mental intimidation, subtle racism is seen in white privilege, institutional practice, and resource distribution.

Both forms of racism are a disease. Those of us inflicted with the disease are in need of healing. And that is what this book is about. Finding healing.

As a first step toward healing, let me tell a story from my life, a story of subtle racism.

Of cigarettes and cowboys

I count Don Guyton among my friends. It wasn't always this way. Once it was worse. Let me tell you how it went from good to bad to worse and back again.

The first time I shook hands with Don Guyton he held an unlit cigarette in his left hand. I remember the brand he favored—Marlboro's. It's one of those imaging brands—cowboys, six-shooters, horses, and the wild, wild West. His cigarettes fit his demeanor. Rugged, strong, capable with his hands, Don is a carpenter, at home with hammers, nails, and lumber. A sawdust cowboy in his own right.

Although he no longer smokes, I will always associate Don with the smell of burnt tobacco curling through humid air. We spent many hours sitting across from each other in smoke-filled rooms. More hours than I wished at the time. Fewer than we needed.

Funny I should remember his smoking so poignantly. The cigarettes didn't tear us apart. In spite of myself, I was impressed with the way he shared his cigarettes. Don freely offered them to those who lacked the means to purchase their own. He shared his addiction, yes, but with an unconscious generosity I could only hope to imitate.

No, it wasn't the cigarettes that tore us apart. Neither was it our beliefs.

Most of the time Don wore a tight T-shirt and blue jeans. Usually the shirt carried a social justice caption, often having to do with the death penalty. Don and his girlfriend Opal were actively involved in the New Orleans anti-death penalty movement. As an ex-offender himself, Don was well aware that while the criminal justice system seldom brings justice to anyone, the death penalty never does.

We were both opposed to the death penalty, supported the homeless, and were convinced that the current political system had long ago bypassed the poor. At the time, we had somewhat differing views of the values of the free market system. He maintained that anyone who hustled quick enough and kept open a sharp eye for business could support a family comfortably. I had all sorts of ideas about the inherent sins of capitalism. Both our beliefs have shifted somewhat since, but even then we spoke openly about our differences.

Somewhere along the way, something happened. Somehow we got off track. To understand the force of subtle racism that derailed us so abruptly, I have to go back to the beginning.

To understand racism, you always go back to the start.

Across the river

Cheryl and I arrived in New Orleans in late June of 1987 fresh from college, only half a year into our marriage. We had accepted an invitation to work with Mennonite Central Committee (MCC). As half of my assignment, we were to live with homeless men on the west bank of the Mississippi River. Along with his brother Tyrone, Don had obtained use of a ten-unit apartment complex owned by a Catholic social service agency in the city. In addition to housing the men, they planned to provide training in basic carpentry skills. They called their organization Invest.

Cheryl and I lived in an apartment by ourselves. Three other apartments provided temporary shelter for a maximum of ten men.

The remaining six apartments were used for office space,

rented out, or sat empty in need of repair. Only three of the apartments—our's and two of the rental units—had air conditioners. One of my first tasks was to find fans for the three apartments for the homeless men. Without the limited relief of moving air, the cement block rooms became saunas.

Looking back, I can see what a huge jump we made in moving from the sheltered confines of a small church school campus to the sweat box of "the Big Easy." I wasn't fully aware of all the changes that came with the move. At the time, all I wanted was to perform well in my assignment, and that meant getting along with my supervisor, Don Guyton.

Don, Tyrone, and their families lived about a half-mile from the Teche Street apartments. From the start I envied the relative distance and separation they enjoyed from the ever-present needs of the men in Invest. In addition to attempting to locate a regular food supply for the men and providing late night transportation to Charity Hospital's emergency room, I was called on to mediate arguments, enforce curfews, and encourage job search. Cheryl and I began to escape across the river whenever we could. Even an hour spent riding back and forth on the ferry provided a modicum of much needed space.

It was a taxing, frustrating job. Don and Tyrone tried repeatedly to find construction work, but several substantial contracts fell through when developers found out Invest would be training homeless men and ex-offenders on the job. Outside of a few odd jobs and an ill-fated attempt at starting a lawn mower business, little work came in.

In the midst of all this tension, Don and I quickly drifted apart. I didn't know why, but I had a few guesses. I wrote the following journal entries during the most intense period of our time at 701 Teche Street. The entries refer to several incidents during which it became apparent I was not communicating well with Don and the men. No one came to one meeting I planned. Later on, I asked for a meeting with the Invest board of directors because I didn't think Don was a competent leader.

I am uncomfortable with some of the entries, which speak too loudly of my own prejudice and confusion. But they are also the best witness to the swirl of emotion and culture wrapping around me.

7/11/87 I don't know how to be white in New Orleans.

7/22/87 Don came and took over. He teased the guys and talked like they did. They responded to him and told him details of living together I hadn't even heard of. He is the boss here. I sat back and tried to listen to him tell the men to get their spiritual lives in order. The more I listened, the more difficult it became to tell the difference between flamboyant Don, Don as a member of the black culture, Don, the ex-offender.

7/24/87 Yesterday afternoon, one of the men told me I'd eat fried ice cream if someone gave it to me.

7/28/87 "One thing about Jody. He's always working on something," said one of the men after I told him that I was working to get sheets for the beds.

8/12/87 I am thankful for the services at Charity Hospital, but we were lucky to get out by 2:00 a.m. My presence with one of the men seemed to speed things up. Dear Lord, it makes me so mad that white skin and middle-class articulation yield so much power.

8/18/87 Angrier and angrier I become with Don. So many missed meetings and late arrivals. I learn not to believe what he says after his promises and excuses.

8/25/87 Am I right to be pushing so hard? God, I don't know. I need to spend some more time in quiet today.

And back again

I knew there were forces swirling around me that I didn't understand. Don had changed from someone I admired to my enemy. Our relationship had deteriorated to such an extent that during a meeting of the Invest board of directors, one board member admonished us to trust each other. "Do that, or go home," he said.

Our conflict came to a head one evening when Don discovered the food pantry in disarray. I had refused to clean it up because it was one of the men's responsibility. On August 27, 1987, just two months after we arrived at 701 Teche Street, I wrote this in my journal.

Upon the evening's return, I found field peas and rice gone awry, the place a mess, and Don billowing through the boundaries. We erupted. He told me and I told him and in the telling there was a tautness which for whomsoever fault broke loose. Exclusion, denial, rerouting, and defeat. I cannot work here anymore.

One month later, we had decided to leave the building. I wrote,

Perhaps what concerns me most in our departure is that we leave behind contact which had, at least in a very few ways, bridged cultures.

Less than a month after that, we moved. On the morning of our relocation across the river, I recorded,

Don said two things last night which greatly helped me. He was the initiator and deserves all the credit. (1) Jody, I sure learned a lot from you and (2) I hope that we can always be friends.

As I transported our belongings back across the river, I pondered the events of the last three months and longed to place blame. An ill-defined job description. Inadequate supervision. The humidity. Culture shock. Personality clash. All of them, yes. But also something more subtle. Something I didn't have the eyes to see, the tools to analyze, or the history to understand.

And so began a continuing journey to find the eyes, to gain the tools, and to reclaim the history I needed to understand this subtle racism and begin the process of healing. Foremost, I wanted to understand the role racism played in the coming together and the tearing apart of a white man and a black man.

I knew that racism had contributed to our separation through undue economic pressures. The simple fact that so few jobs were available to a small, African-American construction firm like Invest intensified their struggle to make ends meet. If Invest had had a regular source of income, we might have been able to spend time learning to work together. Even so, I suspected my desire for control would have been expressed differently if Don had been white.

As I thought more about what had taken place, I realized that our different cultural backgrounds and the assumptions we carried about work, time, relationship, and personal responsibility were also affected by subtle racism.

This racism was bigger, more complex, and ten times more stark than anything I had imagined. Yet I also knew I would continue to flail my way through other cross-cultural interactions if I didn't begin to try and understand it. Like most people who find themselves in such situations, I longed for healing.

As we continue in this journey to the river, we will examine in more detail why this story turned out as it did. This will mean asking some questions about who controlled the resources, who had the privilege, and what assumptions each of us carried into our relationship. It will also mean working with a definition of subtle racism. Most people working to undo racism use the definition, "Racism is equal to race prejudice plus power." This may not make sense now. Later on we will examine it in depth. Understanding the dynamics of racism will help us continue on our journey toward the healing river.

I began the journey out of brokenness but moved toward hope and wholeness. As I said at the start, I count Don Guyton among my friends. Before he left for Connecticut in search of work, we had a chance to talk with each other and regain some of the ground we lost. I feel good about that reconciliation. It gives me hope. But the underlying reality of racism continues.

The journey will be long. I cannot go alone. I need others to travel with me. And as much as I have thrown my lot in with the believers tradition, those "others" need to be the church.

A church in the river

Norristown, Pennsylvania, used to have two more churches than it does now. As recently as 1989, three congregations—African-American, European-American, and Latino—held their own services and paid their own pastors. A year later they combined services and became a single new congregation, Norristown New Life.

In some ways a miracle took place in the course of that year.

In other ways the seeds of this congregational transformation had been planted many years before. Even before the merger, two of the congregations shared the same building. And although all three congregations were separate, they had been meeting regularly for fellowship meals for some time. In fact, it was during one of those meals that Ertell Whigham, pastor of the African-American congregation, had a vision that would eventually lead to the formation of Norristown New Life.

"It suddenly occurred to me," Ertell recalled, "that this is the way it should always be, not just once a month. The kingdom of God is made of many people, not just one kind."

Ertell explored the idea with the other two pastors. All three brought the idea back to their congregations. Within a year the three congregations had sold the extra church building and dissolved their individual structures. One pastor became the pastor for the English speaking members and another for the Spanish speaking members. Ertell became the pastor for administration.

To create a new life together, Ertell explained, they had to begin with the assumption that "we need to accept our ethnic differences, but we must also recognize that Christ is our common denominator." That assumption carried them a long way. In the course of coming together, not one congregation lost a single member.

Of course there have been problems. As Ertell noted, "Some members of the Anglo congregation had a difficult time accepting me as an African-American in the position of pastor of administration. There was also some tension between Colombians and Puerto Ricans. So we leaders realized we had to set an example. We talked about ethnic differences in small groups, but we also brought some of our own members to task for their prejudices."

But despite difficulties, Ertell noted, the experience of coming together across cultures has given him much joy. "There is genuine acceptance as we work across cultures. In this church, we have made it work. We talk about our differences in worship services. We accept those differences and rejoice in them, but we don't accept pride and selfishness."

The first question

The story of Norristown New Life provides us with an immediate answer to one of the first questions we encounter on our journey—"Why be concerned about racism?"

Concern about racism springs first from hope for healing. As members of Norristown New Life demonstrate, it is possible to work together across racial lines and find healing. It is a long journey, but a possible one.

In the new community hinted at in Norristown, it is possible to speak openly about prejudice. Members of the dominant culture can become aware of the intense and unrelenting oppression people of color face. They can examine together statistics like these:

- The average African-American family earns 40 percent less than the average European-American family.
- The black poverty rate is three times as high as the white rate.
- The median European-American household possesses more than ten times as much wealth as the median African-American household.
- Blacks with comparable training and experience as whites earn only 55 percent as much as whites.
- A European-American high school dropout still earns almost as much as an African-American male with two years of college.
- White businesses control 99.7 percent of the U.S. Gross National Product.
- Over half of all European-Americans tend to think of themselves as more intelligent, less lazy, and less prone to violence than African-Americans and Hispanics.
- A full 75 percent of European-Americans think African-Americans would rather be on welfare than work for a living.[3]

Concern about racism also springs from the realization that it affects everyone, both perpetrators and victims. As we will examine in detail in chapter four, society teaches members of the dominant culture from little on up to treat people differently because of their race. North American media, government, schools, and churches perpetuate false assumptions about the superiority of Western models of communication, organization, education, and worship. Individual European-Americans unknowingly accept and come to expect the privilege they receive by virtue of their white skin.

Another reason to be concerned about racism is that demographic projections indicate increasing ethnic diversity throughout North America. After the year 2000, African-Americans, Latinos, and Asians will make up one-third of the nation's students, and approximately 45 percent of the work force.[4] By the end of this century, 53 major North American cities will have populations comprised of majorities of people of color and the largest state in the U.S. will have no ethnic majority. By the year 2020, the number of U.S. citizens who are Latino and people of color will have more than doubled to nearly 115 million while the white population will not have increased at all.[5] Additionally, the United States now has the largest foreign-born population in its history, almost 8 percent. The vast majority of those are Latinos and Asians.[6]

We have no choice but to learn to operate in a culturally diverse society. For people of European descent, this means learning about racism.

Racism with us

I seldom hear racial slurs or jokes, but I do remember a conversation with Nettie. She lives two doors down from us in the top floor of what used to be a roomy town house.

Our apartment is only a block and a half from the main Mardi Gras parade route. During that sometimes raucous, sometimes rowdy, always colorful season, we like to join the crowds in jumping for Mardi Gras cups, beads, and baubles.

One Saturday afternoon, Dylan and I were walking home from a parade. The last float had not yet passed, but even one-and-a-half-year-olds loaded down with plastic loot get tired and need their nap. As we walked past Nettie's house, she asked me to wait for a second. When she came back out, she gave Dylan a small stuffed clown from a previous Mardi Gras parade.

He was quite happy with this addition to his collection. Then almost in passing, Nettie said, "Better get back before those jungle bunnies start marching through." I stuttered and mumbled something about needing to get Dylan home for his nap. Dylan and I returned home.

The target of Nettie's derision unfortunately needs no identification. What does need further examination is my halting, ineffectual response. I could say that she caught me off guard, that I did really need to get Dylan to bed, or that it wasn't that big of a deal. After all, I've since seen Nettie sit on her porch and talk for long hours with African-American members of our neighborhood. Maybe I just didn't hear her correctly. She does mumble after all.

In retrospect, what I regret most is that I did not respond to her racist slur. Silence only expressed acquiescence. It also cheated Nettie out of a chance to examine labels she might not even understand are destructive.

Many of us white people feel uncomfortable when we hear statements like Nettie's. We want to be polite, but we also know we should somehow express our disapproval. The problem is we don't know how. We have little experience responding to racist slurs or jokes.

We also have little experience responding to fears among white people about affirmative action measures. By the time you are finished reading this book, I hope you will be better equipped to understand the role you play in a racist society, to address people's fears about affirmative action, and to respond to racist slurs and jokes.

Together we can find the eyes, gain the tools, and reclaim the history we need to understand racism and begin the process of finding healing. In this way, we can answer the call of the 1989 joint Mennonite Church and General Conference Mennonite Church statement, "A Church of Many Peoples Confronts Racism" (see appendix A). In this way, we can move toward healing.

Scriptures calling us to the river

I will not see an end to racism in my lifetime. I hope to see changes for the better in the next several decades, but the roots of racism have grown deep. Tangled and full of knots, racism entwines itself throughout church and society. The changes we have seen since the days of segregation came about through the concerted efforts and considerable sacrifice of thousands of people. Change now will come about with no less.

I am convinced that lasting change starts in the church. Christians have as far to go, if not farther, than the society around us, but we have the clearer mandate. We are called to be members of a reconciled community.

Scripture is filled with calls to reconciliation. Jesus himself prayed,

> The glory that you have given me I have given them, so that they may be one, as we are one, I in them and you in me, that they may become completely one, so that the world may know that you have sent me and have loved them even as you have loved me." (John 17:22-23)

In Acts, Peter proclaims an important insight: "I truly understand that God shows no partiality, but in every nation anyone who fears him and does what is right is acceptable to him" (Acts 10:34-35).

Perhaps most eloquently of all, Paul reiterates one of the core messages of the gospel in his letter to the Galatians by stressing that

> in Christ Jesus you are all children of God through faith. As many of you as were baptized into Christ have clothed yourselves with Christ. There is no longer Jew or Greek, there is no longer slave or free, there is no longer male and female; for all of you are one in Christ Jesus. (Gal. 3:26-28)

Which way to the river?

I have shared why I am concerned about racism: because I

want to understand what happened between Don and me; because it oppresses my brothers and sisters of color; because we all suffer from its effects; because members of the dominant culture need to understand what racism is in order to function in an increasingly diverse society; because we have not yet learned to respond effectively to racial slurs or jokes; and because Scripture calls us to racial reconciliation.

My guess is that these are some of the same reasons you have chosen to read this book. You may have other reasons. If so, share them. We cannot change racism by ourselves.

In many ways the journey to understand racism is also a journey to the river. It is not a journey across or back again, but a journey to enter in. Only when we enter in as equals will the river heal us. The river is mighty, flowing full of healing, but tinged with the pain of our history. Do not enter lightly or alone.

When I first came to New Orleans to work with Don and the men at 701 Teche Street, I thought my primary task was to cross over to their side, to lose myself in their culture. Either that didn't work or I didn't do it right. I suspect some of both and quite a bit of neither. Understanding the strengths and weaknesses of my own culture and the power I carry on either side of the river comes first. Only then can I hope to enter the river and find healing.

2

Why Is Talking About Racism So Hard?

THE WORD *racism* has only begun to be used in church circles. It is easier to speak of the need for cross-cultural sensitivity or prejudice reduction. Few of us are comfortable speaking about racism as racism. The message sent out is, "Talk about prejudice reduction, celebrating cultures, or managing diversity—but don't talk about racism. It's just too controversial."

For most white people, this racism business is awfully uncomfortable. Should we talk about it? If we do, will we fall into a tangle of *faux pas*? Won't we make other people feel uneasy?

I empathize with people who feel uncomfortable talking about racism. I still do sometimes as well. But that hardly seems reason enough to evade the topic. Just as domestic violence and sexual abuse in pastoral relationships were not talked about for far too long, so too discussion of racism has remained tightly shut in both ecclesiastical and secular closets.

In this chapter, I hope to explore the discomfort surrounding racism. By examining the role of fear, a color-blind stance, and pressure to use the correct word, we may better understand the source of our discomfort. We'll also take some time to introduce the characters from 2 Kings 5.

To that end, let me tell you about another friend of mine.

Discomfort wrapped in red, white, and blue

Fred Richards (not his real name) and I are probably as different from each other as any two North American males of European descent can be. Fred is a member of the advisory board for Survive, a program initiated by Mennonite Central Committee for families of homicide victims in New Orleans. Part of my job as MCC program coordinator included working with the Survive advisory board.

The first time I met Fred I knew we were going to disagree. The advisory board had come together for one of its first meetings on a humid night in early fall of 1991. Soon after I greeted him at the door, Fred pulled out a red, white, and blue handkerchief to wipe sweat from his brow.

I don't object to an occasional show of patriotism. I like fireworks on Independence Day as much as anyone. Yet I've never spent a dime on anything red, white, and blue, much less wiped my brow with a handkerchief of those colors. I later discovered that Fred always carries a U.S. flag-colored handkerchief.

That was just the first of our differences. Later Fred said, "When I see someone who has lost a family member to homicide, I don't see white or black. I just see someone who hurts." It was a compassionate statement, especially when you knew that Fred's eighteen-year-old son was murdered.

Yet I was disturbed. Fred seemed to advocate a color-blind stance, which I consider dangerous and harmful, especially when used to discredit attempts to bring about an ethnically balanced advisory board. So I called Fred to see if he would like to go out for lunch to talk about it further.

I didn't want to call. I don't like conflict. During previous conversations we had talked about gun control, warfare, and welfare. About the only thing we agreed on was the weather. Even then, he called the sky partly cloudy; I said it was mostly sunny.

So Fred picked me up in his jeep. Remember his red, white and blue handkerchief? Fred has a red, white and blue "patriot" decal prominently displayed on the side window of his jeep. I found myself wondering what color his bed sheets were.

During the next hour, Fred told me his life story. He left home when he was fourteen, received an athletic scholarship to a private high school, and played four sports a year until he broke his back in a football game. Subsequently ineligible to play intercollegiate sports, he taught himself polo and played professionally throughout his college career. At the same time he established several businesses, one of which he sold for a sizable profit during his junior year in college. After serving in an elite guerrilla warfare unit of the Marines, he settled down to establish a photo studio.

I relate these details of his life to show that Fred is no slouch. Highly motivated and successful in his field, he is an asset to the work of Survive. I like Fred. I am also aware that even putting all handkerchiefs, jeep decals, and bed sheets aside, we still hold very different views on many issues. In particular, we vary widely in our response to racism.

As our conversation turned to matters of color and prejudice, I became increasingly uncomfortable.

Fred told me the story of how he had tried to help numerous African-American youth get scholarships to a prestigious Southern university, only to see many of them drop out or be dismissed. He talked about urging several of those students "to be a credit to your race." He also advocated for a collegiate-level education program organized to help racial ethnic youth from the inner city "learn to speak right."

I became even more uncomfortable.

Not knowing where to start, I asked a few questions about why the students had left his alma mater. It became apparent that they were feeling extremely isolated in an imposing institution of the dominant culture. The expectations inherent in a disparaging statement like "be a credit to your race," discouraged them. Likewise, saying that inner-city youth did not speak right further demeaned the students.

I didn't tell Fred everything I was thinking but did say some things. I questioned his racial stereotypes. I explained the dangers I saw inherent in a color-blind stance. And I let him know my thoughts about power, privilege, and systemic racism.

To my surprise and pleasure, Fred listened undefensively to

what I had to say. He heard my questions about racial stereotypes. He mulled over my analysis of a color-blind stance. And
he carefully considered my dreams for a racially balanced advisory board in which power is shared equally among members of
the dominant culture and racial ethnic communities. He didn't
always agree, but he listened.

Fred and I continue to hold disparate views on many issues.
We still don't agree on all aspects of racism. But he no longer
stands in the way of structuring our board to share power equally among members of the dominant culture and racial ethnic
communities. We meet regularly to further the work of Survive
and are comfortable talking with each other. After the birth of
our second son, Fred took time out of a hectic schedule to call
me with hearty congratulations.

I have to admit, however, that I'm glad he didn't give us a red,
white, and blue baby blanket.

Completely correct

Having Fred for a friend has helped me realize I don't need
to be quite so concerned that talking about racism will automatically make people feel uncomfortable.

Conversations like those I had with Fred also help me to
come to terms with pressure to use the correct word. Many a
pundit has bemoaned the current environment in which it is
considered inappropriate to refer to people by their skin color,
to celebrate Columbus day, or to cheer for the Washington
"Redskins" or Atlanta "Braves." I have heard people complain,
"It's only a few oversensitive people of color who are causing
this fuss. What does it matter whether I call someone black or
African-American?" Some people seem fed up with having to
search for the currently "correct" term when describing a group
of any type, size, or variety.

I do not entirely understand this impatience. It makes sense
to me to call people by whatever name they choose. That is why
I use very specific terms when describing groups or individuals
by their ethnicity. In this book, I will use "people of color" or "racial ethnic communities" because those are currently the names

most people belonging to those groups prefer.¹ I will not use "minorities" because of the diminutive connotations that term carries.

Likewise, African-American, Japanese, Native American, and European-American and their derivatives will be used instead of Negro, Oriental, Indian, or Caucasian. Occasionally I will use other terms for variety's sake, but my goal is to refer to people by the names they have chosen for themselves, names that avoid the traps set by linguistic racism.

At the same time, I empathize with those who feel frustrated when they are called racist because a term they use is no longer considered appropriate. To be called racist for using a term that only recently went out of style leaves one feeling manipulated, ashamed, defensive. Is it possible to affirm that names are important without falling into correctness traps?

I'd like to suggest that members of the dominant culture let go of anxiety about whether or not they are using correct terms. Having done this, they can learn to know people first as individuals, then as members of cultures rich in history and significance.

Our aim should be to get to know others well enough that the names they use for themselves will be the names we use as well. Along the way, we may also discover we have less need to speak in generalities. As we get to know specific individuals, we use their names. We have less need for "Native American" or "Asian," and more need for "Steve" and "Kim."

A small and silent fear

Charlene, a European-American, worked within the African-American community. She helped set up a program that ministered to drug abusers. Under her capable leadership, local mothers came together and organized numerous activities to keep their children off drugs.

One day a representative of her major funding source asked to interview Charlene for an article about the drug-abuse program. In answer to a question about the community in which she worked, she said, "There are several distinctions about African-

American life. One is that drug abuse is expected. It is not as devastating as it would be to me or you." Her exact quote later appeared in a newsletter widely circulated among donors supporting her work.

A month or so later, Charlene was asked to give a short presentation at a board meeting of this same funding source. She
gave a moving presentation filled with stories from the people
she worked with. Board members thanked her for her work and
moved on to the next agenda item.

At the end of the meeting, an African-American board member came up to talk with Charlene. She had read the article about
Charlene's work and was impressed with the organizing model
Charlene implemented. But she had a concern. The board member explained to Charlene that her comments about drug abuse
in the African-American community portrayed African-Americans as callous, unfeeling people. The comment also placed
Charlene in the position of outside observer and analyst. Furthermore, the use of "you and me" gave the impression that the
audience was all white, an inaccurate assumption that once
again placed people of color on the outside.

Charlene was glad for the board member's honesty. Thinking about the interaction upon returning to her office, she realized many things. First, she had been helped to see her assumptions about members of her organization with new eyes. *Am I really an expert on the African-American community?* she asked herself. *Should anyone be? And do I really want to be an observer? Didn't I
start this work to be with people?*

She also recognized she hadn't gotten over some of her prejudices. They were deep and hard to face. The encounter brought
her face to face with a fear she rarely acknowledged. It was a
small and silent fear that she might one day say or do something
that would reveal the prejudices she knew she carried.

And it had happened. But she wasn't condemned. No one
banished her to the fields of Siberia. She learned from the experience and kept at the work.

Although the names and a few details have been changed,
this is a true story. By no means unique, it represents a fear that
many members of the dominant culture must face when work-

ing across cultures. By giving voice to her fear, Charlene admitted she was no superwoman. She would make mistakes. She would also be more at ease talking about assumptions she carried into her work.

Like Charlene, society bombards us from little on up with the unceasing message that "white makes right." We cannot escape those lifelong influences overnight. Yet with God's help, we can engage in a process of healing. Mistakes will take place, but we can learn through them. We don't have to sit down, immobilized by fear.

No one likes to be called a racist

There's another part to that fear. One I have not dealt with quite as well. It can be summarized by the statement, "No one likes to be called a racist."

I have written and talked about racism often. My work with families of homicide victims, public middle school students, and residents of public housing developments in New Orleans forced me to grapple with the effects of racism in the society around me and the racism in me. Yet I still find myself hesitating when someone asks me what I do for a living. My hesitation does not come from having to explain for the thousandth time what a Mennonite is (and is not). I hesitate because I feel a bit uncomfortable telling them I spend my time working to dismantle racism.

Occasionally the inquirer asks more. Why racism? Isn't it great we don't have that problem in the church? But these questions and the ensuing dialogue are rare. Usually the response I receive is a close cousin to the blankest of stares. I accept those stares with a certain sense of relief. *Thank goodness*, I say to myself, *I don't have to talk about racism again.*

I try to imagine what is going through people's minds when I tell them what I do. Maybe it goes like this: *Racism. Oh, no. He's probably one of those angry reactionaries out to make us all feel guilty. He's probably going to condemn me because I'm white. He's probably going to call me a racist.*

As we'll examine later, it is important to understand what we mean by "racism" and "racists." But even using a definition of racism that includes an understanding of systems, power, and white privilege, I still don't like being called a racist any more than anyone else. As much as I try to disassociate myself from all the volatile emotions that come readily attached to the racism label, at some level or the other they remain. So I understand those stares I receive.

I'm not satisfied with the stares, however. I want to work toward the day we can talk freely and openly about prejudice and racism. To that end, I try to acknowledge my fears and invite other members of the dominant culture to do the same.

No, I do not want to be called a racist. But if someone places that label on a group to which I belong, I hope I will take time to discover what is meant so I am better equipped to work at undoing racism.

Only the color-blind welcome a monotone world

A common response to racism, whether subtle or overt, is to advocate for a color-blind stance similar to the one Fred Richards proposed to me. I have come to believe such a stance is potentially destructive. I can understand the well-meaning intentions that lead people to speak of being color-blind. But such an unrealistic approach merely ignores the richness of peoplehood found throughout our world.

A brief story about a North American church worker on leave from an assignment in El Salvador demonstrates this point.

Owen Lapp had worked in Central America for many years. While there he met and married a woman from El Salvador. Soon after their wedding, they arranged a speaking tour through the U.S. West Coast.

People who met Owen and his wife, Alejandra, were impressed with them. They lived simply, spoke powerfully, and responded compassionately to the world around them. One of their hosts in Portland recalled the caring way Owen addressed a homeless man on the street. "He spoke to him like he was as important a person as a long-lost friend," their host recalled.

A few weeks later, when they had reached San Francisco, their hosts had set up a busy schedule of interviews and public speaking engagements. When the day was finally over and Alejandra and Owen sat in their host's living room, a comment was made about one of the interviewers they had spoken with. Their host referred to the "tall man from Channel Four."

Owen didn't recall the interviewer. Then their host mentioned that the interviewer was African-American.

Owen responded, "I don't notice people's skin color."

In a follow-up interview several weeks later, Owen's San Francisco host said, "I remember wishing I could be as color-blind as he. To walk through the world, completely unaware of people's skin color.

"Now I am not so sure. I think it is not only impossible but also undesirable to ignore the many shades of skin color God has created. Not only do I want to recognize skin color for all the splendor and variety it adds to our world, I want to recognize the many cultures that people I meet bring with them to our interaction."

At times, I've wished I was as color-blind as Owen. So have many others. A recent university conference on racism was entitled "Eyes wide open and color-blind." It's a catchy phrase, but unrealistic.

We have been given a world dappled with wonderful diversity. We miss a valuable opportunity to appreciate the richness of ethnic diversity in this country if we aim for color-blind sight. Insisting on a color-blind stance only supports forces that ignore ethnic distinctions outside the dominant norm.

I am not proposing, however, that we describe people by reference to their ethnicity and skin-color alone. The more we get to know people of all ethnicities, the more they and we can appreciate each other as individuals with specific gifts and shortcomings.

I now notice people's skin color much more than I used to and am much more conscious of their ethnicity. I welcome that increased consciousness but acknowledge that a whole new set of challenges comes with it. What associations do I attach to different skin colors? Are my responses different for people of different skin colors? Am I aware of the privileges that come to me because of my skin color?

Uncomfortable questions, yes. But I would rather deal with that discomfort than live in a monotone world. A monotone world is drab, filled with only one color, devoid of variety, slower to adapt, less able to respond to a variety of circumstances.

The discomfort is our hope

A small and silent fear. Completely correct. No one wants to be called a racist. Only the color-blind welcome a monotone world. Has examining these points brought us closer to talking about racism without discomfort? I hope not. Let me tell you why.

We talk easily about things we like. We find it more difficult to speak of things that cause pain. If we blithely spoke of racism with no hesitancy, no feelings of discomfort, it would indicate that we had become anesthetized to the effects of racism. Because we are uncomfortable talking about racism, we are still sensitive to the pain it creates. Our discomfort indicates our willingness to engage in action for change.

When we talk about racism with at least some sense of discomfort, we recognize that things are not as they should be. More African-American males should not be in prison than in college. People of European descent should not be given automatic privilege simply by having white skin. Almost 45 percent of all African-American children and nearly 40 percent of all Latino children should not have to be poor.[2]

As a child of the biblical Sarah and Abraham, as an adult member of the redeemed community, I recognize my discomfort. That discomfort is my hope. My hope leads to healing. Until we find healing for the ravages of racism in our hearts, our schools, our political institutions, and our churches, may the discomfort and the hope remain.

Of leprosy and legionnaires

The Scripture story of Naaman's healing from leprosy (2 Kings 5) provides a strong metaphor for the journey that I and all members of the dominant culture must take to find healing from the effects of racism. The account offers all the metaphors a writer on racism could ever wish for. A healing river, a clash of cultures, prejudice, long suffering, an irascible prophet, and an uncertain participant. Let's take a moment to familiarize ourselves with the story.

First the setting. The story opens in the land of Aram between 800 and 840 B.C., most probably in its capital, Damascus. Aram was not so much a political entity as an agglomeration of Aramean people, but it held great strategic power, concentrating much of the wealth and culture of the area.

Now the characters. Naaman was a much respected, highly decorated military officer in the Aramean army. Most biblical accounts say Naaman was afflicted with leprosy. However, scholars agree that the term "leprosy" in this context could also refer to any number of molds or fungi in buildings and an equally varied group of human skin diseases. At any rate, Naaman knew he needed healing even though the disease did not keep him from succeeding at his job.

Elisha was the prophetic successor to Elijah. He was known for many miracles, including filling oil jars in the home of the widow (2 Kings 4:1-7), restoring the son of a Shunammite woman to life (4:8-36), and making an ax head float on water (6:1-7). As prophets go, Elisha wasn't of the more friendly sort. This is the man who called in two bears to maul forty-two youths after they vexed him with taunts about his bald head (2:23-25). A venerable man, to be certain, but really rather cantankerous.

A nameless young Israeli girl, captured during one of the frequent battles between Aram and Israel, was servant to Naaman's wife. We don't hear much about her, but she provided a vital link to Elisha's healing powers.

The Old Testament account doesn't give the names of Naaman's wife or the king of Aram (though historical records indicate he could have been Hazael). But a close reading of previous chapters of 2 Kings reveals that Joram son of Ahab was the king of the northern kingdom.

The plot is straightforward. The servant girl tells her mistress of the healing powers of Elisha. Naaman's wife passes the information on. Naaman gets permission from King Hazael to go to Israel. Naaman visits King Joram, who refers him to Elisha, who then tells him to wash seven times in the river Jordan. After some initial hesitation, Naaman follows the instructions and is healed. He professes his belief in the God of Israel and, after a brief encounter with a foolish servant of Elisha, returns home to Aram.

At first glance, the story of Naaman and Elisha seems to have very little to do with a discussion of racism. Yet the story provides a strong metaphor for the journey that I and all members of the dominant culture must take to find healing from the disease of racism. The story shows how white people of faith can wash in the river and find healing from racism.

Scripture stories have often come alive for me by re-examining passages from the perspective of one of the main characters. For purposes of this book, we will spend most of our time in the shoes of Naaman. To do that, we must agree to one basic tenet. White people in North America are afflicted with racism. As we will see in chapter six, we are afflicted in a much different way than are people of color. Yet we are stricken with the disease of racism just as Naaman was stricken with leprosy.

You may shrink from this assertion, yet I am convinced that in those places of silence and truth inside of us where we hear God most clearly, we know racism is an evil which afflicts us. We will explore in later chapters just how white people are afflicted with the disease of racism and need healing. We will also share stories from people of color oppressed by racism. And we will get to know Naaman through further Bible study and the telling of stories from the Mennonite church in North America.

Naaman's shoes are hopeful ones. Naaman was washed by the river Jordan. Naaman found healing.

Come to the river. Be ready to find healing.

3

What Is Prejudice?

Perhaps THIS CHAPTER isn't really necessary; we're all too familiar with prejudice. Everyone has a story to tell.

But do we know the difference between prejudice and racism? They are frequently used interchangeably in a variety of settings. Proceeding on the assumption that most of us aren't familiar with the difference between the two, in this chapter I'll concentrate on answering the first part of the question, "What is prejudice?" To that end, I'll tell stories of prejudice in contemporary settings, examine the fundamentals of prejudice, present a definition of prejudice, and look for the presence of prejudice in scriptural accounts.

Of bosses calling "coward"

Sam Johnson spoke out against the war in Iraq. In addition to supporting the many conscientious objectors who had refused to participate in killing, Sam condemned the actions of the allied forces as unjust and immoral. His comments later appeared in the paper and were shown on television.

After each comment aired or appeared in print, he received anonymous, angry, and sometimes threatening phone calls. One day, a short snippet appeared on the morning news. After the news had aired, Sam left the hospital following his night shift.

As he was about to get on his bike to go home, Sam's boss charged up to him, yelling at the top of her lungs. After she had seen him on television, she immediately searched him out. She accused him of trying to murder her son, who was on the front lines in the Gulf. By undermining support at home, she said, he placed her son in jeopardy. She called Sam a coward.

A menacing crowd gathered around Sam, but he was able to get away before anyone could harm him physically.

Sam went home and shut his door tightly. The anger, hate, and prejudice had rocked him to his core. Even though he knew he wasn't a coward, and that his supervisor was afraid she would lose a loved one fighting in Iraq, the name still stung.

Fortunately Sam received support and positive response from others in his faith community. One man, who Sam at first thought was out to harass him, called to let Sam know he should not be intimidated. The caller had undergone similar harassment during the desegregation era. Sam's supervisor was reprimanded for her unprofessional behavior.

I am thankful that I rarely come in direct contact with someone who has prejudged me. Although I experienced some minor harassment during the Gulf War for statements I made in support of conscientious objectors, I never faced the intense prejudice Sam did. When I do come in contact with people like Sam's boss, my defenses rise up. I am at a loss to respond. I want to say that I am more than a stereotype; I am a multifaceted person, loved by God, too complex to be described by one word alone. A Christian, a man, a person of European descent, a writer, a runner, a father, a husband, a lover of books. Each of these descriptions might describe part of me. None describes all of me.

Everyone has been a victim of prejudice. Perhaps someone held prejudices about you because of your height, weight, or hair color. Maybe his or her prejudice was aimed at your physical condition, age, gender, religion, political views, nationality, or race. The list could go on; too often it does.

Unfortunately, the reverse is also true. Everyone can tell a story of having acted out a prejudice. I remember all too well the time I slammed a door in the face of another member of my Sunday school class. With all the superiority my thirteen years could muster, I walked away from this "dorky" kid. What's worse, I denied having shut the door in Curt's face. I said I didn't see him.

We are afraid of losing our jobs, of the unknown, of a different worldview. The hurts of personal loss, past experience, and disappointment undergird our fear. Then we act on our prejudices. "Backward" or "ignorant" people do not have a monopoly on prejudice. The story of prejudice is the story of the world; everyone can tell it.

The color of my underwear

Above all, prejudice requires the creation of an in-group and an out-group.[1] I remember an out-group experience in Miss Best's first grade class. One slow Friday afternoon at Winterbourne Elementary School, Miss Best devised a game to keep us attentive until the dismissal bell rang. Although I no longer recall the exact purpose of the game, it involved going to the front of the room if you were wearing a certain color of clothing.

She began with some less common colors, orange and purple, then started into the browns and whites and so on. After the first several colors had been called, only a handful of my classmates stood at the front of the room. How I wanted to be among them. To stand proudly in front of everyone else. To belong to the in-group. To have the color of my clothing called out.

The next color she called was black. I popped up from my desk and walked proudly to the front of the room. I was in. I was up front. But then Miss Best asked, "Jody, what are you wearing that's black?" I had so desperately wanted to be included that I figured I had to be wearing something black. It didn't appear that I did, however, so I blurted out, "My underwear."

I had to return to my desk, humiliated. Fortunately my brown belt came in handy the next go round.

I tell this story not only because it brings a smile these many years later, but also because it shows how important a sense of belonging to the in-group is to us all. Miss Best didn't want to create divisions within her class. She just wanted to keep us interested on a slow Friday afternoon. Some in-group/out-group designations start out just as innocently. We enjoy being with people like us. The problem comes not in free association but when individuals benefit because of inclusion in a group or others are denied benefits because of exclusion.

Moving from the distressing to the horrific, once the defining characteristics of the in-group and the out-group are determined, they are often codified and given the force of moral sanction or law. For example, though the U.S. Congress has passed legislation making reparation payments to Japanese-Americans forced into concentration camps during World War II, it remains legal to round up members of any out-group in a time of emergency. Title II of the McCarran Act gives the president the power to declare an "internal security emergency" in a time of "insurrection" at home.

The president may also authorize the attorney general to arrest and detain people without charges or warrants. These "insurrections" might be "civil rights disturbances, peace demonstrations, or any other disruption which the president alone might interpret as a qualifying emergency."[2]

Japanese-Americans were rounded up without the legal help of the McCarran Act. How much easier it now would be for the president to round up Iraqi-Americans in a time of war or African-Americans in a time of urban rebellion. History provides the painful lesson that people in power will not hesitate to use prejudice as means to an end.

Another fundamental of prejudice deals directly with the names we call others. One of the first lies our culture teaches us is summed up in the playground rejoinder, "Sticks and stones may break my bones but names will never hurt me." Names do hurt. Not only do they cause emotional damage, they also serve to create a destructive one-dimensional image of the other. Even as we remember the words of the psalmist, "I praise you because I am fearfully and wonderfully made" (Ps. 139:14), we know that to call another a harmful name is a sacrilege.

God has not made cowards or dorks. Neither has God wrought Commies, fags, whores, close-minded fundamentalists, or weak-kneed liberals. Such names deny the fullness of creation. They cheapen the intricate complexity of humanity that includes both the sordid and the saintly. Such names have no place in the body of believers.

The names of prejudice also reveal the weaknesses of the name-caller. Sam's boss was deeply frightened at the possibility of her son's death when she called Sam a coward. When I shut the door in Curt's face, I was responding to an unacknowledged fear that I was dorky too.

Prejudice also makes the false claim that differences are detrimental to the health of the community. When we call someone a weak-kneed liberal we make the inference that the world would be a better place if all weak-kneed liberals weren't here. Only a short and ragged jump stands between such thinking and mass extermination of any out-group. Hitler didn't start out killing Jews and homosexuals. He began by building up a vision of a homogeneous race devoid of differences.

God has made this world a place of variety and splendor. Our individual life experiences add to that diversity. In the midst of these differences, conflict will occur. Even without prejudice, it takes a lot of work to build up community. By creating space to share our stories and beliefs, we knock the feet out from under prejudice. This space may not make conflict disappear, but it gives us a much better chance of appreciating and benefiting from the diverse world God has given us.

Before we look at more formal definitions, one more observation about prejudice. Prejudice is so very dangerous not because it is irrational, but because of its fundamental rationality. People come to hold prejudiced views through live experiences and socialization that make prejudice seem rational to them. The worldviews of prejudiced people are skewed, distorted, and nearsighted, but they define truth as the individual knows it. To move beyond prejudice, we need to acknowledge that prejudice seems rational from within such views. Only after understanding prejudiced worldviews from within can we hope successfully to propose alternatives.

Defining prejudice

We've looked at how prejudice creates in-group and out-group distinctions, depends on name-calling, thrives on denied weakness, and appears perfectly rational to those who are caught up in it. Now for a definition.

Prejudice is what it sounds like. As linguists note, the word *prejudice* can be traced to the Latin equivalents of *pre* and *judge*. Here's the definition I have found most helpful: *an opinion, thought, or feeling based on assumptions made about an individual without getting to know him or her.* This is not as precise a definition as one found in a dictionary, but it helps me concentrate on the relational elements of prejudice.

For example, the *Random House College Dictionary* (1982) defines prejudice as—"1. an unfavorable opinion or feeling formed beforehand or without knowledge, thought, or reason; 2. any preconceived opinion or feeling, either favorable or unfavorable; 3. unreasonable feelings, opinions, or attitudes, especially of a hostile nature, directed against a racial, religious, or national group." These are probably more accurate from a linguistic perspective. I don't find them as helpful, however. Keep both definitions in mind as we move on.

Knowing the definition of prejudice does not make me more resistant to its effect, but it has helped me examine racism. As I noted earlier, prejudice is only part of the definition of racism.

He came from Galilee

He was born amidst a mongrel people. In the area where he lived, visitors from faraway lands came and sold their wares. Most left. Some stayed. Those that made this place their own married, raised families, and blended in. It wasn't that difficult. In such a place, Phoenicians, Syrians, Arabs, Greeks, Orientals, and Jews all felt at home.

You couldn't ask for a more cosmopolitan region. It had passed through Assyrian, Babylonian, Persian, and Macedonian rule before coming under Roman jurisdiction. International trade routes crossed the region, bringing more than those bent on commercial interests alone. And so cultures mixed, blended, and learned from each other.

But there were drawbacks for the Jews living in the area. The

Pharisees looked down on them because they were supposedly ignorant of the law. Those old Sadducees thought the Jews from Galilee weren't exactly rigorous in their attention to the detailed rules of temple worship. For that matter, educated Greeks and Jews regularly mocked Galilean Jews because they had a tendency to slur guttural sounds. On occasion, they were not allowed to recite public prayers in the synagogue.[3]

You knew a Galilean when you met one. In addition to the way they butchered proper speech, they were poor. Dirt poor. Poor in every way that mattered. They were stubborn and backwards, not to mention impure. In a word, inferior.[4]

Jesus knew prejudice.

He was from Galilee.

Prejudice in the Bible

Before setting down to write this book, I had never thought of the Bible as a book full of prejudice. Yet as I began to reread different biblical accounts, I discovered that even as the Bible is a story of the people of God with all their faults and failings, it includes many incidents of prejudice.

As demonstrated above, Jesus grew up among a people habitually derided and looked down upon. Jesus knew what it meant to hear a slur of prejudice, to be discredited even before he had a chance to prove himself as an individual. In the gospel according to John we hear Nathanael say, "Can anything good come out of Nazareth?" (John 1:46). Nazareth, located in the heart of Galilee, obviously carried a profoundly negative connotation.

Continuing our chapter two exploration of the story of Naaman and Elisha (2 Kings 5), several prejudices are immediately obvious. The first we see in the war between Aram and Israel. No wars can take place without prejudice and plenty of it. Only prejudice allows soldiers to meet on the battlefield and try to obliterate each other. The many hateful, angry names that surface during wars help dehumanize the enemy by creating one-dimensional monsters "deserving" death.

It used to be common practice for victors of a war to take

slaves. The 2 Kings account implies no injustice in the taking of a young Israeli girl to serve as servant to Naaman's wife, yet the institution of slavery requires a heavy undergirding of prejudice. How else can people force people to work without pay or freedom?

U.S. history bears witness to how the church can get caught up in heinous crimes of prejudice. Many a church leader espoused religious dogma which claimed that African-Americans were less than human, thereby allowing slave holders to treat their "property" as they chose, without fear of moral condemnation. Even those who treated their slaves kindly or gave them an education were still heavily involved in a racist system. As we'll soon discover, being nice is never enough.

The text does not indicate how Naaman treated his slaves. We can only assume he adhered to normal expectations of his society, which precluded harsh physical treatment of servants. Yet in spite of what were no doubt heavy prejudices against his wife's servant girl and the children of Israel in general, Naaman went to Elisha to find healing.

After he had been told what he must do to be healed, Naaman resisted washing in the Jordan. Though the Jordan was a muddy little creek compared to the clear rivers of Damascus he was accustomed to, Naaman's complaints indicate something deeper than simple dislike of muddy waters. His prejudice comes through when he whines, "Are not Abana and Pharpar, the rivers of Damascus, better than all the waters of Israel? Could I not wash in them, and be clean?" (2 Kings 5:12). Notice he says "better than," not "cleaner than." "Better" carries a value judgment and moves the complaint into the realm of prejudice.

Naaman's servants eventually convince him to wash in the Jordan. He overcomes his prejudice and comes out a healed man. But let's not jump ahead to the healing too quickly. We still do not fully know the nature of the disease.

The Bible is filled with stories of people who were both victims and perpetrators of prejudice. We need look no further than the actions of the twelve disciples. The disciples rebuked those who brought the children for Jesus' blessing (Matt. 19:13). They were surprised to see Jesus speaking to a Samaritan woman (John 4:27). These same twelve beseeched Jesus to send the woman of Canaan away when she sought healing (Matt. 15:23). Prejudice toward children, Samaritans, and Canaanites influenced the disciples' responses in each instance.

It may also be helpful to identify with people in the Bible who have been victims of prejudice, to reread the texts from their perspective. How did Joseph feel lying in the bottom of the well after his brothers had tossed him there, possibly to kill him? What feelings ran through David's mind as he waited in the fields for Jonathan to come with a report about Saul's behavior toward him? Did Shadrach, Meshach, and Abednego feel more than the heat of the flames as they walked toward the furnace? Did they also feel the heat of prejudice?

What did the woman with dropsy feel before Jesus healed her? What about the woman who was going to be stoned for adultery or the Samaritan woman at the well? And what of the Gentiles who wanted to follow Christ after his resurrection but faced opposition from the established Jewish population?

These stories show that Jesus came to bring healing to those who were victims of prejudice as well as to those oppressing others by their prejudice. Why else would he have surrounded himself with a band of followers who held so many prejudices of their own? Both groups needed healing. Both groups could tell stories of having been both victim and oppressor. Like us, they needed to be washed in the healing river.

4

What Is Racism?

IN THIS CHAPTER I will try to answer the question, "What is racism?" by examining a definition of racism, the pervasiveness of racism, racism in institutions, and assumptions behind racism. While the ideas in this chapter can stand on their own, they make most sense after a careful reading of chapter three. Together the two chapters provide a foundation for further exploration of white privilege in the context of racism.

At Washington and S. White

Dan Boudreaux (all names have been changed) is the director of a large social service agency in New Orleans. In 1989, he underwent triple-bypass heart surgery. The surgery went well but he needed to remain in the hospital for observation and recuperation.

On the way to visit his father, Dan's son Bill was involved in a serious accident. Although no one was hurt, both cars were seriously damaged. The police arrived soon after.

Bill told his side of the story. He had gone through the light at a safe speed when it was green. The driver of the other car maintained that Bill had run a red light. At the time of the accident, the other driver had no license with him and was using the car without permission of its owner.

A taxicab driver came up and testified that he had seen the accident. He declared Bill was in the wrong. Bill knew the taxicab driver could not have seen the accident. He didn't appear on the scene until well after the accident had taken place.

Bill was given a ticket. The other driver was not. Bill's insurance rates doubled.

One other dynamic played into the unfolding of events. Bill was European-American. The police officers, the other driver, and the taxicab driver were African-American.

A Mission Hill murder

On the night of October 23, 1989, Charles Stuart called the police on his mobile phone to report a horrible crime. As sirens blared and the press gathered in the Boston neighborhood known as Mission Hill, he told the police how a black male had entered his car, demanded cash and jewelry, and shot both him and his pregnant wife, Carol.

Carol died. Charles recovered from his stomach wound. Their son, Christopher, lived only seventeen days after having been delivered by emergency Caesarean section.

The press trumpeted the story across the continent, "Innocent couple attacked by crazed convict." Charles became an overnight hero, a symbol for the nation of courage in the face of violent crime.

The Boston police undertook a major sweep of black neighborhoods. In addition to randomly questioning black males, they encountered on the street, they arrested William Bennet, an African-American with a sizable police record.

As William's indictment was being prepared, Charles Stuart committed suicide. Only a short while earlier his brother had admitted his role as an accomplice to Charles' plan to murder his wife. It became apparent that Charles had shot his wife, wounded himself, and then called the police.

William Bennet was released.[1]

Defining racism

I have purposefully chosen two stories that bring race relations into high relief. Of the two incidents, one tells the story of race prejudice. The other, the story of racism. Neither is pleasant. Both are uncomfortable. But only one gives witness to the force of racism.

In the last chapter, we defined prejudice as "an opinion, thought, or feeling based on assumptions made about an individual without getting to know him or her." Prejudice, however, is only part of racism. The second part is power. In other words, racism is equal to race prejudice plus power.

As basic as it may appear, this definition results from years of reflection and deep analysis on the part of many people working to dismantle racism across North America.[2] When racism is defined as race prejudice plus power, it leads us to the conclusion that people are not racist simply by holding prejudices. Everyone holds prejudices. Everyone has been affected by prejudice of some sort.

Only people with power to enforce their prejudices can be racist, however. In North America, "there is only one racial group which has the power to impose its will upon other groups."[3] The group with this power consists of members of the dominant culture, people of European descent—white people.

This definition helps clarify the difference between incidents of race prejudice and racism. Bill Boudreaux was a victim of race prejudice. He is certain the taxicab driver chose to testify against him because he is white. At first he felt that the police officers were also out to get him, but on later reflection he concluded they were responding as objectively as they could in a tense situation. The only witness except for Bill and the driver of the other car was the taxicab driver. The cab driver's testimony held sway.

According to our definition, Bill was not a victim of racism. Certainly the taxicab driver held momentary influence over Bill, but this was not power in the sense that counts beyond the confines of the intersection of Washington and S. White Streets.

Compare the influence the cab driver's falsehood had on Bill's life to the influence Charles Stuart's falsehood had on William Bennet's life. William wasn't at the site of the crime. Charles didn't even point him out. All he said was that a black man entered his car. That was enough to set off a huge police dragnet. Not only was William arrested without hard evidence linking him to the crime, but hundreds of other African-American males were randomly questioned and harassed on the street. All because a white man said a black man committed a crime.

Certainly there is a difference of degree between the two stories. One involved a car accident, the other a homicide. But even that cannot account for the difference in power held by the cab driver and Charles Stuart. What would have happened if Charles and Carol had been persons of color and Charles had said a white man attacked them? I know of no place in North America where a similar response by the police would have taken place.

The effects of race prejudice, regardless of who holds it, create damage. Without power behind it, however, the damage is limited and immediate. Racism is far more pervasive, backed by immense institutions and fueled by often unexamined assumptions.

It is a bit like the difference between a fire in a desert and a fire in a forest. Race prejudice is like a fire in the desert. It can burn and destroy, but it will almost immediately run out of fuel. Racism is like a fire in the forest. It also burns and destroys, but the fuel to feed it runs on endlessly. A desert fire can easily be quenched by a few people. Only a deliberate and costly effort by many people can put out a forest fire. The extent of damage caused by a desert fire can be quickly assessed. A forest fire causes damage that will only be fully understood in years to come.

Racism is pervasive

The results of racism extend far beyond the criminal justice system. In the next chapter we will examine how race prejudice plus power oppresses people of color. For now, a few statistics will suffice to demonstrate just how pervasive racism is.

Racism exists in the work place. According to a 1992 study of public and private sector employers in Detroit and Los Angeles,

20 percent of the employers stereotyped African-American males as lazy and violent. Similarly, a 1991 Cook County, Illinois, study demonstrated that "employers view inner-city workers, especially black men, as unstable, uncooperative, dishonest and uneducated."[4]

Lest we think that racism is isolated to a few employers in major metropolitan centers, two million instances of racially motivated housing discrimination occur every year.[5] Likewise, whites have eleven times the wealth of African-Americans.[6]

Similarly, as early as 1986 the U.S. Commission on Civil Rights concluded that violence against Asians is a national problem. Some examples of the abuse include Hmong refugees beaten and harassed in Philadelphia; Cambodian families' homes torched in Revere, Massachusetts; a Chinese American stabbed in New York by teenagers shouting, "Let's get these Chinks out of here!"; two Japanese students beaten at the University of Wisconsin by a group of drunken whites who uttered a racist remark; and Native Americans murdered in Jersey City, New Jersey, by a group called the "Dotbusters"—whose sole aim was to terrorize Native Americans until they were forced out.

These statistics and incidents need no explanation. They bear stark witness to the presence of overt racism.

The following two stories reveal the results of racism in other institutions. Unlike the preceding stories and statistics, these stories point to a more subtle manifestation of racism.

Sparrows and robins know not to mix

The experience of the Fellowship of Hope, a Mennonite-connected congregation in Macon, Mississippi, highlights the power given to white people in an institutional context.

In early 1986, four couples came together for a Bible study. Two of the couples were African-American. Two were of European descent. They each had three children.

They had big plans—a credit union, counseling programs, tutoring, youth work. They found common ground talking about the problems of the community. As Levi Hatcher, an African-American founding member, noted, "We were tired of sitting around doing nothing, just watching the community go to pot."

Although only four couples met during that first year, their gathering had already begun to threaten people.

"We kept hearing the sparrow and the robin story. We hadn't heard it for years. 'The birds do not mix. The robins are very proud of themselves being robins. The sparrows, they are the way they are, but they know not to mix. God has ordained it,' " recalled Larry Miller, a European-American founding member.

They continued to meet, others joined them, and in the process they discovered just how much of a spectacle they had become. On August 29, 1988, someone burnt down the house they had been meeting in.

Not long after the fire, Levi was approached by another African-American church member who said, "Our church has to be right and good because white people are involved."

Levi replied, "It has to be right for that reason?"

"No, it has to be right because the public perceives that it is right, because white people would not be involved in anything that's not right," was the response.

Such assumptions about the "rightness of whiteness" had to be dealt with as they sought to build community. One night those assumptions came out in the open.

Since the fire, they had built a new church building and their church life had settled down. Soon after they moved into the new building, Levi, church council chair, called a council meeting. At that time, the Fellowship of Hope had a five-member church council made up of three whites and two blacks, three of them male and two female.

Larry Miller also sat on the council. It had been primarily at his urging that the council had been set up. "I grew up with a church council model," he said. "Every church had a church council. The pastor did what they said."

But Larry had begun to question the appropriateness of that model. What originally appeared like the only right way to make decisions now seemed a useless layer of bureaucracy.

As the council members chatted in the church kitchen waiting for Levi to return from another part of the church building, they informally batted ideas back and forth. Levi returned and asked what they had been discussing.

Larry responded, "Well, we've decided to do away with church council."

Levi replied, "Okay."

After minimal discussion, they accepted Larry's decision and began to talk of ways to implement the idea.

Lying in bed that night, Larry thought about what had taken place. Whether or not the decision to disband the council was the right one for the church, he had made it. As the only white male on the council, everyone had automatically deferred to him. "I realized I was that big booger I thought I was," Larry said. "I felt that is how it always works. White people end up with the power."

In an ensuing discussion over the racism discovered in the meeting, Levi added, "I've seen extended arguments in the church in which all it took to end a discussion was the opinion of one white person. When I tried to say something to cool the flames, the argument wouldn't end."

Lucille Hatcher echoed this reality, "If a white person says something, it's going to be heard and done. You have the privileges to get the learning and skills in leadership that put you at an advantage."

What is so unusual about the Fellowship of Hope is not that they have to struggle with racism in their midst, but that they are able to talk about it so openly. As another member, Carmen Walker, noted, "We [white people] need to try and dig up as much of that racism out of our minds as we can. We'd much rather keep it hidden. Yet we need to let God clean it out of us. It's a continual process."

A bridge to the black community

In the mid-1980s, Maureen Peats-Bond worked with Mennonite Central Committee in Atlanta, Georgia. During that time she was the only African-American member of the Atlanta service unit.

In reflecting on her time in Atlanta, Maureen recalled an incident that highlights the power given to white people, even well-meaning white people actively involved in social justice work.

Maureen wrote, "MCC Atlanta was and is quite involved in many social justice issues. Often I was the only black in the room. Too often, people thought I should and would single-handedly be their bridge to the black community."

No thought was given as to why there were so few African-Americans involved in the social justice organizations to begin with. Instead the focus was on Maureen's ability to connect with the local African-American community. The people with power attempted to define her role without asking her what she wanted it to be.

Maureen's experience with racism is not limited to the South. While growing up in Ontario, she had to face similar race preju-dice and power on a daily basis. That racism extended even into the confines of the church.

"Although my family attended the same church for almost two decades, no one could tell my sisters and me apart. We had a pact. If people thought I was one of my sisters, or vice versa, we would respond with the appropriate information. For example, my sister Monique has a fabulous voice and sings at conventions and in churches. When people asked me where and when I was singing next, I gave them Monique's itinerary. It wore us down to give in to the prejudice that 'we all looked alike.' "

The members of Maureen's church did not take the time to get to know Maureen and her sisters as individuals. Although they look no more alike than other siblings, they were grouped together as the "black girls" at church. People at Maureen's con-gregation could get by without learning to recognize different facial characteristics in another ethnic group. Members of the dominant group had the power to determine which ethnicities deserved attention and which could be relegated to the margins of church life.

Maureen's story and that of the Fellowship of Hope demon-strate how subtly race prejudice and power can be realized. Even well-meaning church people in the church get caught by assumptions they have carried with them their whole life. When backed up by power, those assumptions have damaging results.

Of assumptions, seemingly innocuous

We read of specific incidents of racially motivated violence or egregiously discriminatory hiring practices and shake our heads at the ignorance of people who take part in such action. Far more prevalent, however, are incidents of subtle racism undergirded by seemingly innocuous assumptions. As members of the Fellowship of Hope have discovered, assumptions about who makes the decisions need as much attention as the decisions themselves.

In preparation for a speaking tour on racism, Cheryl and I took in 1991, Cheryl wrote about an experience that helped her become more aware of racist assumptions she carries with her.

Susan is my co-worker. It is from her that I learn most about my own racism because Susan is honest with me. She lets me know when I've done or said something typical—for white folk.

Once I was present when Susan discovered a mistake Debbie, her supervisor, had made. When Susan asked Debbie about it, Debbie acknowledged the error but insisted it wasn't a big deal. After Debbie left, Susan looked at me. "Isn't that just the typical arrogant attitude? They don't pay me enough to put up with that."

She meant typical white attitude. I asked, because I thought she was being unfair. But then I realized that if Susan had made the same mistake as her white supervisor, she would have been accused of being careless or even incompetent.

Susan helped me see the subtle double standard I have for blacks and whites.

A mistake for a white person is an isolated incident. A mistake for a black person points to a larger character flaw.

The double standard assumes the worst of black families. I am surprised, therefore, when I meet an intact African-American family at the clinic. I am surprised when an African-American teenager comes in for a physical because he just got a job. I expect girls to come in pregnant at age fifteen.

I didn't really think about this double standard until I noticed that I tend to look down on white people who come to this low cost clinic. I think the reason is that I expect white families to do better. If they are coming to us, they must be really bad off. (All names have been changed.)

I can tell far too many stories of white assumptions leading to racist action. Here are two vignettes from our time in New Orleans.

I attended a conference several years ago held at an Episcopal church parish house not far from home. During a lunch break, I sat on the front porch to enjoy the cool air of early spring. After a few minutes, I stepped back inside to get something to drink. As I went in, a fellow conference participant stepped out.

A little while later, just as we were about to begin our afternoon session, the church security guard came in to ask if anyone had been sitting on the porch during lunch. He went on to explain that a neighbor across the street had called to report a "suspicious" looking man lounging on the steps of the parish house. We later discovered that the neighbor was not concerned by my bearded appearance on the porch, but by the appearance of an African-American man, my fellow conference attendant.

The neighbor assumed I belonged while the other conference attendant did not. I was "normal." The African-American was "suspicious." As it happens, there were far more people of color at the conference than white folk. I was really the suspicious one. Fortunately the guard saw the tragic humor in the situation as much as did the rest of us. We all had a good laugh.

In an even more graphic portrayal of the role assumptions play in undergirding racism, members of the St. Thomas Housing Development tell a story of a television reporter's coverage of a local homicide.

A woman was decapitated by her husband in a neighborhood just two blocks away from the Garden District, a wealthy, all-white neighborhood. During the evening news, the reporter never referred to that neighborhood. In fact, she described the murder site as being "near" St. Thomas. St. Thomas is about a mile away. Neither the murderer nor his deceased wife had any association with St. Thomas other than that they, too, were African-Americans.

The reporter assumed there had to be a connection between the homicide and St. Thomas, an area that often gets media attention for violent crime. Because she did not take time to examine her assumptions, the residents of St. Thomas were wrongly associated with a heinous act. Without meaning to, the reporter reinforced prejudice about the people of St. Thomas.

A racism to call my own

The definition of racism I have used throughout this chapter, race prejudice plus power, makes sense to me. Even after working with it for several years, however, it continues to unsettle me. If this definition is true, and my life experience leads me to believe that it is, then I am part of a racist system.

All around me I see power being used to act out prejudice. I see store guards randomly accosting young, African-American males when someone reports a theft. I see people of color working at the unsavory jobs of opening sewer lines, cleaning hotel rooms, and busing tables. Meanwhile whites supervise the sewage and water board employees, own the hotels, and manage the restaurants. I see all-white Mardi Gras krewe members throwing special treats to white women and their children while ignoring the African-American children right next to them. I see police immediately arresting a suspect in the murder of a white man while hundreds of black homicides go almost unnoticed.

As much as I want to say I am different from the store guards, hotel owners, and Mardi Gras krewe members, I receive the same tacit privileges they do. I seek to be antiracist by refusing to patronize commercial establishments that are obviously racist and by working to empower African-American families of homicide victims. Yet it is impossible to extract myself completely from this racist system.

What's more, if I apply the definition to myself, I have to admit I am a racist. I am prejudiced. Not as blatantly as a member of the Ku Klux Klan. Not as noticeably as those who regularly use racial epithets. But I have not yet shaken those deep, almost unconscious assumptions of prejudice.

For example, one June morning several years ago I unlocked our front door to begin my morning exercise, only to discover that someone had shattered the passenger side windows of the two vehicles we used in our MCC work.

After cleaning out the broken glass, reporting the incident to the police, and arranging for someone to install new windows, I reflected on what had taken place. One of the first things I realized was that I had conjured up a specific image of the perpetrators, even though I had no way of knowing who they were. My mind's eye saw two young, African-American males in their late teens quickly breaking the window with a pry bar.

I do not want to write that image. It speaks too loudly of who I am, of what assumptions I make, of my prejudice. Whether or not this image is backed up by statistics of vandalism in our city, whether or not I can refer to personal experience to reinforce that image, and whether or not I will ever find out who actually broke the car window, the fact remains that I carry a prejudice about African-American male youths.

And I am powerful. Not powerful in the sense that the president of the United States is powerful. Not powerful in the same way that the CEO of a large corporation is powerful. I am powerful in that I have access to institutions, education, and resources that are routinely denied people of color, if not blatantly, then subtly. Most of those institutions are staffed and controlled by people like me, people who view the world in the same way I do, who carry similar dress codes and understanding of time, who look like I do.

Gender plays into the power I receive to a certain extent. As a male this society gives me power and opportunity that is only beginning to be offered to females. However, a European-American female receives many of the same benefits I do. She receives more benefits than does an African-American male. Salary differentials alone witness to this disparity.

I am prejudiced. I have power. I am a racist. That realization is not only unsettling, but downright threatening.

Nobody likes to be called a racist.

To be sure, the point of defining racism as race prejudice plus power is not to bandy about a whole new set of emotionally charged and guilt-laden labels. The twin demons of labels and guilt spawn only immobility and hopelessness. I know of no one who has gone on to work at undoing racism because of being told she or he was a racist.

Yet an understanding of white people's race prejudice and power is essential. In North America, people of European descent benefit greatly from a racist system. Most of the time we do not seek out the power given us. Mostly we do not act out our prejudice or do specific harm to any one individual. We don't have to. The system does it for us; we don't have to lift a finger.

I do not believe it is ultimately crucial whether or not members of the dominant culture use the term *racism* to describe the combined effect of their race prejudice and power. It is far more important that members of the dominant culture seek healing for themselves and for the systems that deny power to people of color. Only by actively seeking ways to challenge the assumptions behind "white is right" can we hope to be healed of the affliction of race prejudice plus power.

Neither good nor bad, just a disease

When I am most honest, I know I carry race prejudice. I don't carry it because I want to or because I am a bad person. I carry it, as do most members of the dominant culture, because I have been taught by countless advertisements, history lessons, housing arrangements, news reports, and even scriptural exegeses that white culture is the norm. I have been taught that white culture is at least subtly, if not dramatically, better than other cultures. The learning is deeply ingrained into the fabric of my daily interactions, communication, and society as a whole.

In the next two chapters I'll look more closely at the different forms racism takes and how it afflicts both people of color and members of the dominant culture.

Throughout the remainder of this book whenever I use the word racism I will be referring to the definition of race prejudice plus power. If you read a statement such as, "All white people

benefit from racism," I am saying that all members of the dominant culture are given power, whether they ask for it or not, to
act out prejudices. I am not saying that all white people secretly
support the activities of the Ku Klux Klan or the Aryan Nations.

I am also not saying white people are bad because they are
given that privilege. It just happens. We may speak of the systems that deliver that privilege as bad. There may even be cause
for examining the ethical nature of our collusion with those systems. Yet I have come to believe that an ethical examination of
racism is best directed toward our response to racism and white
privilege. It is more important to hold each other accountable for
our response to racism than to label each other racists.

It may be helpful to think of racism as a disease, like leprosy.
No one wants it. Few people actively try to get it. Having the affliction does not indicate ethical misconduct. But the contagions
are everywhere. The disease of racism is epidemic within members of the dominant culture in North America. Not because
they want to be sick, but because the disease is so contagious.

The disease of racism may not be immediately obvious, especially if we live in communities where everyone is afflicted with
the disease. As time passes, the symptoms of the disease become
more obvious. As we come in contact with those not so afflicted,
our debilitations become more apparent. A desire for healing
wells up inside. We move toward the river.

Naaman wanted healing. He serves as an example for those
of us afflicted with the disease of racism. Although he initially resisted an invitation to wash in the Jordan, he overcame his hesitation. Maybe he realized that healing waters are often muddy.
We don't always find healing where we would like it.

Naaman knew he had a disease. Perhaps that is how he provides the best model for us. It takes courage to admit to a disease.
It takes humility to accept treatment. Naaman seems to have had
both. The first step in understanding racism is accepting that we
white people are given power to act out our prejudices. Only
then can we move toward healing.

Back to 701 Teche St.

When I told in chapter one of my relationship with Don Guyton, I wrote of the many forces that contributed to our separation: differing cultural backgrounds; disparate assumptions about work, time, and relationship; the economy; personality clash; personal failings; and a misplaced struggle for control.

I then asserted that racism played the lead role in our separation. I didn't explain that statement in full. I'll do so now.

Racism worked in very specific ways to undermine my time at Invest. If Don and I had been able to talk about the racism confronting us, we might have been able to work together for a longer time. We might still have come to a point of separation, but I'm convinced we would have saved a good bit of pain and stress.

For starters, racism came into play in how we handled our different cultures. My culture has given me assumptions about how to run a meeting, what it means to be on time, how to relax, which foods are delicious, which distasteful. The problem was that I assumed my ways were inherently correct. If Don was fifteen minutes late for a meeting because he had taken time to talk with one of the men, he had failed. I even kept a notebook to track every time Don was late.

Racism also came into play as economic pressures constantly pummeled Invest. Don and his brother Tyrone were hampered in their search for work because of racist prejudices against African-American ex-offenders and homeless men. Educational resources, personal contacts, and easily obtainable bank loans support the work of dominant culture contractors. Don had to struggle constantly, eventually moving out of state, to gain access to any of the resources other contractors took for granted.

The educational system also affected the work of Invest. First of all, educational opportunities were not readily available to Don or Tyrone. It was not that they would be denied access to seminars or business courses because of their skin color. Instead, racism was inherent in the set of assumptions upon which almost all the business colleges and seminars were built. They were built around people who had the job flexibility and financial resources to take time off to attend expensive seminars. Most of the people teaching and taking the seminars were members of the dominant culture.

Fortunately some small business resource centers have been developed, but they are not adequate to shore up the bigger holes left by the public educational system. At Invest, I was given the task of teaching fractions to the men in the program. Two weeks of intensive work brought only one of them up to rudimentary proficiency in adding fractions. This was not due to mental disability; two weeks of my teaching simply could not make up for huge inadequacies in the public education system.

In New Orleans, as in many other North American cities, the public education system is underfunded, inadequate, and dangerous. Despite valiant attention by creative educators, the schools are simply not receiving enough money. It is not unheard of for all the teachers in a New Orleans high school of 3,000 students to rely on a single hand-cranked mimeograph machine. Text book condition, class size, teacher salaries, and physical plant condition go down from there. An excellent, adequately funded, 90 percent white private school system exists side by-side with the almost all-black public system.[7]

And so racism threw another log of frustration on the growing pile between Don and me.

Likewise I had difficulty trusting Don to lead the work of Invest. I remember thinking he was not working hard enough to make Invest succeed because he had not stayed up all night to prepare a grant after working all day on a construction project. I later discovered he had only been informed of the grant application process that evening. Here again, an African-American was kept out of the circle of information about grant deadlines. The assumptions behind who should know about the grant left Invest outside the loop.

I didn't pause to consider the high level of respect that Sontee, Melvin, Edward, and the rest of the men in the program held for Don. If Don had been white, I would not have been so critical of his leadership abilities.

Of course, personal failings came into play. I can be too rigid and legalistic in my demands of other people. Don does not always follow through on tasks as well as he should. We both like to be in control.

But I have worked with people with failings similar to Don's. People have worked with me and been aware of my failings. Almost all of those people have carried a set of assumptions similar to my own. Almost all have been white.

Something bigger, more complex, and ten times more stark than personal failings alone contributed to our separation. That something was racism—racism made visible in the economy, educational system, cultural assumptions, grant-making, and evaluation of leadership competency.

Racism is not the final word

Yet as I said at the beginning, I count Don Guyton among my friends. As we worked to find some degree of reconciliation, we caught a glimpse of the new community Paul writes about in Ephesians.

> So then you are no longer strangers and aliens, but you are citizens with the saints and also members of the household of God, built upon the foundation of the apostles and prophets, with Christ Jesus himself as the cornerstone. In him the whole structure is joined together and grows into a holy temple in the Lord; in whom you also are built together spiritually into a dwelling place for God. (Eph. 2:19-22)

I am given most hope by Paul's assertion that we are growing. Paul refers to a process, a movement, a journey. As we discover the nature of our disease we can move toward the river in search of healing. Just as Naaman's healing didn't happen immediately but only after seven trips to the Jordan, our healing from racism will not happen overnight. Healing from the disease of racism takes place in the course of a lifetime rather than an afternoon, so tenacious is the disease .

But I believe healing *will* finally come, and in three forms: healing from race prejudice, healing for institutions that give tacit power to white people, and healing of assumptions that keep "white equal to right." The healing takes time, but with God's help it can occur.

As we begin to understand the dynamics of racism, to appreciate cultures other than our own, to share power equally, and to create new structures open to members of diverse cultures, we must also realize that race and culture do not define the totality of our being. God has made us male and female, singers of sound, thinkers of thought, makers of motion.

Together we are believers in a risen Lord. Together we will be set free to claim our inheritance across all lines of race and culture. The healing river awaits.

5

How Does Racism Afflict People of Color?

IN THIS CHAPTER we will look at stories and examples of how people of color are afflicted by racism. Notice the wording here, "afflicted *by* racism." This is different than the question of the following chapter, "How are white people afflicted *with* racism?" I have chosen these two prepositions for a specific purpose. "By" connotes action upon a group. For example, "The spectator was hit *by* the baseball." Racism is a force acting upon people of color in many ways similar to how a baseball strikes a viewer in the stands.

In this chapter, we will examine how the disease of racism afflicts people who do not have that disease, who aren't on the playing field of racism. In particular we will look at how racism is expressed in history, language, culture, and institutions. In the next chapter, we will look at how racism afflicts people who have the disease, those on the playing field, those *with* racism.

I don't make this careful distinction to sow seeds of discord between members of the dominant culture and people of color. We all know there are far too many barriers to reconciliation already. Neither am I suggesting that one culture or ethnicity is better than any other.

I make a distinction between those who have the disease and those who do not for a specific reason. I am trying to underline once again that the current distribution of power and privilege in North American is on the side of people of European descent. The systems that most actively perpetuate the disease of racism are overwhelmingly controlled by white people. Those systems operate on cultural assumptions of white people, making racism a white problem.

The underlying message of this chapter is that the oppression of people of color is far greater than anyone who has not experienced that tyranny can imagine. I hope the following stories and examples will open a small window into the world around us. A world oppressed by racism. As we journey to the healing river, may we who have never experienced that oppression catch a glimpse of it, however fleeting.

Let me now tell two stories without commentary or transition. They stand on their own.

While looking for chicken à la king

On his way home one night in 1980, Gregory Bailey stopped at a supermarket in Dover, New Hampshire. Since it was late, the front doors were closed; only a side door remained open.

Gregory entered. As he began to shop, he noticed someone at the far end of the aisle. Otherwise, the store was empty. Gregory soon became aware that the person was watching him, so he moved to the next aisle. The person followed. Gregory moved back. The person started to move with him, but stopped when it became apparent Gregory had noticed.

"This sort of thing happens quite a bit," Gregory said with a sigh.

One night he and his wife went to a restaurant in South Burlington, Vermont. After they were seated, a woman in a nearby table asked the waiter in a loud voice if she could have another table. She said it was too smoky where she was sitting. No one in the restaurant was smoking.

"After thirteen years of an interracial marriage, you learn to be territorial," Gregory remarked. "You try to do things in the same area where people know you and are used to you. It's sort of strange living in a country that places limitations on my travel," he added.

The racism Gregory encounters isn't always overt. On several occasions, he and his wife have looked at apartments for rent. When one of them goes alone to check out an apartment, the owners are interested in renting it. When they show up together, the apartments have already been rented.

When the car breaks down

Ron Tinsley is a graphic designer who works for Mennonite Central Committee in Akron, Pennsylvania. For one year he lived with Linda and Titus Peachey, other MCC staff. Ron is an African-American. Linda and Titus are of European descent.

One night at the supper table, Linda and Titus discovered how different their life experience is from Ron's.

That morning, Titus took an MCC car on a trip to Washington, D.C. On his return home, the car broke down because of a computer malfunction. Titus had to call for assistance from the rural community of York.

As they sat around the supper table, Titus told Ron about his trouble with the car. Ron had used the same car the night before on a trip to Philadelphia and had not returned until late in the evening. He was relieved the car had not broken down for him. Titus teased Ron a little bit for wishing him bad luck, but then he realized that there was more to Ron's concern than he had originally thought.

"If that car had broken down for me late at night out there in the country," Ron said, "and the police had found me, I would have been in big trouble. They would have thought I had stolen the car. If I had gone to a house to ask for help, I probably would have been met with a gun."

Inside the jungle gym

As I heard each of the stories above, I realized again that Gregory's and Ron's life experiences are vastly different from my own. I can think of only one incident similar to the stories they tell.

One morning recess during my fourth-grade year at Hawthorne elementary school in Elkhart, Indiana, two friends of mine and I were rounded up and forced inside a jungle gym. The only other white boys out at recess were involved in a racially motivated fight on the other side of the playground. No teachers noticed us trapped inside the jungle gym, since they were busy trying to break up the fight.

Although no one hurt us, I remember the taunts and threats that the African-American boys ringing the jungle gym threw in at us. It was a frightening, scary time.

When recess was over and the fight stopped, the teachers finally noticed us trapped inside the jungle gym and let us out.

I value that memory, long since healed of any pain it may have once carried. It provides me a small window into the world of cages. Through that window, I catch fleeting glimpses of the oppression people of color regularly face.

Yet I can think of only one such racially motivated incident. The people I spoke with while preparing this chapter had no trouble describing numerous incidents of racism in their lives—which were merely the most obvious symptoms of an entire system of institutionalized racism.

Two different types

Stan Maclin pastors Jubilee Fellowship in Richmond, Virginia. As an African-American, he has reflected on his experience with racism and the experience of those with whom he works. He notes two different forms of oppression against people of color in North America. Stan differentiates between victims of racism and victims of victimization.

Victims of victimization take easily recognizable forms. For example, when people have been victimized for generations, hope becomes harder and harder to come by. The oppression can become internalized. The offspring of that generation are left feeling isolated, alone, and hopeless because all the systems seem stacked against them. Stan notes, "Victimization leaves young people with no moral sense against robbery or being put in prison."

Likewise, Stan points to the victimization that takes place in the welfare system. He describes a system that penalizes people who try to leave it. Benefits are immediately cut off with little or no time for transition. "The welfare system has taken the male out of the home by reducing benefits when couples stay married," Stan adds.

Stan's observations about the welfare system are not limited to people of color, since the majority (nearly two-thirds) of U.S. households receiving welfare benefits are white.[1] But a disproportionate number of people of color receive those benefits (39 percent of black households and 27 percent of Hispanic households compared to 9 percent of European-American households). These people must thus struggle with the dependency the system encourages.[2] A brief story shows how this form of victimization takes place.

In 1984, New Orleans hosted the World's Fair. Many large corporations helped promote the event and promised city officials they would hire hundreds of local workers. And they did.

For the hundreds of openings, hundreds more showed up. People were hungry for work, and for once jobs were available. Several women from the St. Thomas housing development applied for jobs. After waiting in long lines and filling out multiple forms, they were hired. They found someone to take care of their children. They went to work. Although their pay wasn't fantastic, they were able to earn more than they received from Aid for Families with Dependent Children (AFDC).

Some bought a few nice things they had long waited for—an easy chair; a kitchen table; a television. With the promise of steady work for at least a year, the small monthly payments did not seem overwhelming. And they shouldn't have been.

But one short month into their new jobs, they were laid off. No explanation other than, "Sorry, we misprojected." Even before lower than anticipated attendance forced other layoffs, these jobs were cut. Some analysts have speculated that the companies never meant to hire as many people as they did. City contracts forced them to hire—but couldn't keep them from laying people off.

What of the women who had worked so hard to break the cycle of dependency? Three long months passed before they could reapply for food stamps and AFDC benefits, sort through the paper work, prove they had been laid off, and get their benefits in the mail. Of course the television, easy chair, and kitchen table had to be returned. For those three long months no money came in, no food stamps supplemented what little grocery money could be scraped up, no new job opportunities arose.

They took a risk and got a job. The support stopped. They lost their job. It took a long time to get the support back. Why try again?

And so the system of welfare creates victims of victimization.

Now for the remainder of this chapter, we will look at the oppression people of color experience as victims of racism. This form of oppression can be harder to see. It is even more directly tied into systems. It is even more pervasive.

In the history books

History writers in North America have long portrayed people of color as nonexistent or as passive recipients of the forces of European expansion. This kind of racism takes many forms describing racial ethnic groups inaccurately, excluding mention of significant achievements by people of color, giving credit to European-American leaders for movements begun in racial ethnic communities, and using language that warps perception of historical events.

Since the examples included here are by no means a complete list, we need to develop skills that will allow us to read historical narratives with new eyes. To that end, keep in mind three questions while reading this section and other historical accounts.

The first question identifies the speaker, "Who is telling the story?"

The second question examines the players in the story, "Who is actor and who is acted upon?"

The third question encourages comparison, "How is the story different from other stories about the same event, especially those stories told by people who 'lost'?"

By asking these questions, we become more than passive recipients of historical narrative; we learn to examine these stories for the racism so often embedded within.

Inaccurate description of racial ethnic groups is glaringly evident in descriptions of Native Americans. This diverse group called North America home for centuries prior to the arrival of the first European settlers. Yet many of the words and phrases used to describe them lack any respect. For example, the Washington Redskins football team still depicts cartoon stereotypes of Native Americans on their football helmets. Additionally the name itself is derogatory. "Redskin" suggests that the only thing important about Native Americans is the color of their skin. Other baser names are not worthy of mention.

Another way the portrayal of history aids racism is through exclusion of significant achievements by people of color. I only recently was made aware that Garrett A. Morgan, an African-American, invented the traffic light and the gas masks used in World War II. During the Civil War, Robert Smalls and three companions captured a Confederate gunboat, the *Planter,* and turned it over to Union forces. Norbert Rillieux invented a key component in processing raw sugar to fine white crystals.

The list of African-American contributions goes on. Matthew Henson codiscovered the North Pole. Charles R. Drew developed modern blood bank techniques. Jane C. Wright was a pioneer in the use of chemotherapy. Daniel Hale William was the first surgeon to perform an open-heart surgery that saved a human life.[3]

Likewise, Native American nations have contributed immensely to the world community. In the area of agriculture, Native Americans developed and processed potatoes (Incas raised 3,000 different varieties), used fertilizers (bird *guano* in South America and fish heads in the north), and practiced extensive hybridization. In politics, the U.S. federal system is based on the

League of Iroquois. This league of diverse Native American nations even included elements not instituted in the U.S. until years later, such as voting rights for women.

Modern medicine provides another example of Native American contributions. Treatments for scurvy, malaria, and constipation come from remedies practiced by Native Americans while Europeans were still experimenting with bloodletting. The Aztecs knew about the circulatory system long before European scientists understood it. Native Americans even treated skin wounds with a substance similar to petroleum jelly long before Europeans discovered its curative properties.[4]

In yet another example of the racism embedded in historical accounts, European-American leaders have been given credit for movements begun in racial ethnic communities.

The credit given to Abraham Lincoln for ending slavery provides a direct example of this facet of racism. As historian Vincent Harding notes,

> While the concrete historical realities of the time testified to the costly, daring, courageous activities of hundreds of thousands of black people breaking loose from slavery and setting themselves free, the myth gave credit for this freedom to a white Republican president.[5]

At the time of his emancipation proclamation, Lincoln had hopes of resettling the freed slaves in Haiti and throughout Central America. He only issued the emancipation proclamation after the Confederate states refused his invitation to return to the Union with their slave systems intact.

Lest we think Lincoln was pushed by his Northern white constituency to set the slaves free, Harding quotes Senator Lyman Trumbull of Illinois, "Our people want nothing to do with the Negro. We do not want them set free to come in among us."[6] A combination of political and economic forces led Lincoln to his decision, but it was the African-Americans held in captivity who struggled for years for their own freedom and saw that it was brought about.

Robert Moore provides a fourth example of historical racism.

He describes how historical narratives often warp our perception of events. Moore states,

> Euro-Americans are not described in history books as invading Native American lands, but rather as defending their homes against "Indian" attacks. Since European communities were constantly encroaching on land already occupied, then a more honest interpretation would state that it was the Native Americans who were "warding off," "guarding," and "defending" their homelands.[7]

Such language choice is not accidental. It helped to justify the European-American conquest, virtual enslavement, and mass genocide of Native Americans.

Out of our mouths

As a writer, I have been most challenged by the ways in which language is used to perpetuate racism. A system all its own, linguistic racism afflicts people of color through verbal association, character description, and Christian imagery. While this list is not complete, it will bring us into a consideration of how we choose our words and describe the world around us.

The English language is rich with imagery. Metaphor, simile, trope, and a host of other figures of speech enliven conversation and add sparkle to literature. Certain figures of speech, words, and phrases perpetuate negative associations with people of color, however. Some are immediately obvious: Indian-giver, Chinaman's chance, yellow-bellied. Some need closer examination such as "denigrate," to sully or defame, which is derived from the Latin root for "blacken." In this way blackness is subtly associated with defamation.

And so we come to one of the most prevalent associational patterns in the English language, black and white. Time and time again black is associated with all things negative: black-hearted, black outlook, blackball, blacklist, blackmail, black sheep of the family, black magic. White is associated with goodness and purity: whitewash, white lie, white flag, virginal white, white house, white magic. While there are minor exceptions to both patterns ("in the black" and "white elephant" or purely descriptive terms like "white oak tree, "white hot metal," "black cherry tree," and "blacktop pavement"), the overwhelming majority of terms set up a positive and negative division.

In my writing, I have made a conscious effort to move away from black and white imagery. Although initially I thought it would be difficult to come up with other images, this has not been the case. There are countless other options available, as different as fire and ice, spearmint and garlic, Istanbul and Indianapolis, Mt. Everest and Death Valley, and granite and pudding.

Of course, by avoiding black and white imagery I do not change the absurdly evil connotations of black or the ridiculously pure connotations of white. Those changes only come through time and concentrated attention to common practice. But I am confident those changes will come to pass as we continue to learn more about the subtle nature of linguistic racism.

Children's literature and television programming also can contain linguistic racism. My two brothers and I used to act out intricate dramas of adventure and intrigue. Occasionally racial stereotypes would enter into our Thespian productions. The stereotypes were easy to mimic. We had seen them on television, heard them on the radio, and read them in books.

If we wanted to represent an Asian character in our drama, a few stock phrases set the scene: "Honorable so and so," "Confucius say," "roots or ruck," "very solly," and "flied lice." Likewise with Native American characters: "Boy not hide," "Indian take boy," "Heap big," "Many moons," or simply grunt out "Ugh" or "How." In addition to being inaccurate and demeaning, Robert Moore points out that using these phrases makes people of color "seem less intelligent and less capable than the English-speaking white characters."[8]

A fourth way in which linguistic racism afflicts people of color is found right in our very midst, in European-American churches. Other resources examine in depth how racism is played out in worship style, leadership choice, and educational materials.[9] For purposes of this chapter, I would like to draw attention to two aspects of this form of racism.

Joseph Barndt refers to a particular manifestation of the black/white dichotomy discussed above when he notes, "linguistic racism becomes magnified a hundred-fold when words such as 'white,' 'bright,' and 'light' are used to speak of God, purity, sinlessness, and forgiveness, and when we use words such as 'black' and 'dark' to speak of sin, evil, death, and the devil."[10]

It is probably not possible to remove every reference to God as light since that particular image occurs so often throughout Scripture. Yet becoming aware of the connotations that come with repeated use of these terms, especially when juxtaposed against "black," will push us to consider alternative images.

In a related aspect of racism, pictorial representations of Jesus in North American churches have consistently portrayed him as having European-American features. While I hesitate to suggest that it is inappropriate to depict Jesus or God in the clothing and facial characteristics of one's cultural setting, it is important to recognize that Jesus of Nazareth was a Galilean.

Recent scholarship has begun to demonstrate the cultural and ethnic ties of the Near East with Africa. Cain Hope Felder and other theologians have catalogued in detail the many geographic, cultural, economic, and ethnic ties between the earliest biblical people and the people of Africa. As Felder notes, even though in biblical times there was no sense of race as we perceive it today, Jesus and his people "clearly resembled many individuals who would today be identified as African-Americans."[11]

Several artists have drawn pictures of Jesus in a style more closely approximating how he may have looked. It may be helpful for churches of the dominant culture to place some of these pictures in prominent settings in church buildings.

We have already examined several institutions that perpetuate racism through subtle assumptions and overt practices, most notably the church and schools. Examples from earlier chapters included law enforcement and business. Here we will return briefly to the workplace, then examine racism in the military.

When a workplace becomes diverse

When a workplace, whether police station or business office, has made steps toward increasing diversity, attention still needs to be paid to interpersonal behaviors and power distribution. Rita Hardiman lists ten ways members of the dominant culture often behave toward people of color in the workplace. Her list includes making allowances for low productivity because of low expectations, expecting a racial ethnic co-worker to act as a spokesperson for her or his entire race, not giving honest feedback for fear of being labeled racist, and creating job assignments with little power or impact[12] (see appendix B for a complete list).

Hardiman makes two main points. The first is that simply putting diverse people together on a work site does not automatically end racism. Each person brings a whole set of assumptions, prejudices, and levels of power to intra-office relations. If no attention is given to spelling out those assumptions, reducing prejudices, and equalizing power, disaster awaits.

The second point Hardiman makes is that members of the dominant culture need to be continually on the lookout for paternalism in the course of their interaction with people of color in the workplace. In our eagerness to encourage diversity, double standards may develop. In addition to not encouraging fellow workers to excellence, white co-workers may treat their fellow office-mates with kid gloves, almost as if they were breakable, a curiosity on display.

Overcoming racism is hard. Whether in the office place or church, it takes time, courage, and commitment to make diverse workplace settings viable. But it can happen. We'll examine some how-to's in chapter eleven.

From the Gulf

It may seem strange to include a section on racism in the military in a book which assumes Anabaptists as one key audience. Most members of Anabaptist churches are already familiar with the shortcomings of the military. Yet because the military is often lifted up as a viable employment opportunity for racial ethnic youth, it is essential that we take time to look at the military and expose some of the racism found in this institution.

As with much of racism, the following story is about the way we see the world. It is about guns, blood, and the sands of Saudi Arabia. The story begins in Germany.

During the fall of 1990, Cathy and Andre Gingerich Stoner were working with the Military Counseling Network in Germany. The network was founded to give support to members of the armed forces stationed in Europe who were questioning their involvement in the military.

A few months after the United States declared war on Iraq, Andre and Cathy were inundated with phone calls from GI's troubled about their possible deployment to the Gulf. Andre and Cathy noticed that many of the calls from African-American GI's expressed a concern not present in other calls.

"To understand the sense of alienation we heard from the African-American soldiers, you have to remember that the Gulf War came on the tail of major cuts in armed forces in Europe. Over a hundred bases were closing," Andre stated. He went on to note that "many African-Americans felt that the Pentagon didn't want to send them back to the U.S. where no jobs were available, so they decided to send them to the front lines where they'd be killed."

At the time, the Pentagon was projecting high casualty rates. The soldiers' fears were also grounded in the statistical reality that higher percentages of African-Americans are sent to the front lines than to other parts of the military. Keeping in mind that people of color account for less than a quarter of the total U.S. population, during the Gulf War almost half of troops stationed in the Gulf were people of color.[13] Similarly, the Jobs with Peace Campaign reports that African-Americans comprised 30 percent of the ground troops during the Gulf War while they were only 12 percent of the total U.S. population.

Andre recalled a conversation he had with an African-American soldier who had experienced numerous hassles in the army, many of them race-related. "To compound the situation," Andre said, "he had been picked up for driving while under the influence and had a few other potential charges pending. However, none of the charges had been pressed. They weren't going to prosecute him until after he had been sent to the front lines. If he made it back, then they would put him in the brig."

Back in the U.S., Cathy and Andre had a chance to speak with an African-American army reserve officer. "As the war was starting, she and a lot of her friends had the same impression: the Gulf War was just another way to get rid of people of color."

Reflecting back on the many conversations he had, Andre stated, "What struck me was the sense of alienation that the comments expressed. Based on their experience, African-Americans in the military felt used once more, this time in a most cynical manner. They were deeply alienated from the men who gave the orders and from U.S. society which cheered on the war."

Such incidents may seem incompatible with the fact that an African-American officer has been chief of staff of the U.S. armed forces. Yet similar accounts have surfaced time and again.

Other statistics underline the fact that simply placing a person of color in high office will not change the systems that perpetuate racism. For example, racial ethnic members of the military make up half of military stockades and a high percentage of those in the lowest military jobs, receive a disproportionately high percentage of less than honorable discharges, and (once they leave the military) have an unemployment rate twice that of white veterans.[14]

Not to imply

Before moving on to the next chapter, I want to make clear that the discussion of racism above is not meant to imply that the lives of people of color are defined by the racism they experience. Far from it. The dynamics of racist oppression do not define the lives of people of color any more than my affliction with racism defines the totality of my being. All of us must deal with racism, but it does not constitute who we are as children of God.

I also don't mean to suggest that people of color are passive victims of racism. In addition to organizing to resist the disease, people of color make valuable and significant contributions to church and society.

6

How Does Racism Afflict White People?

IN THIS CHAPTER, I will try to answer the question, "How are white people afflicted with racism?" The answers to this question are important to me. Inasmuch as I want to find healing, I need to know how I have been afflicted. I want to understand this affliction not only because it affects me, but also because it affects people I care about very much. This affliction is the malady of my people. It is the disease of racism.

Fishing for diversity

When Stanley Kropf was a young boy he used to go fishing. There were four kinds of fishing he knew about—deep sea, fly, trolling, and nigger fishing. "I had no idea 'nigger' was a pejorative term. It just meant sitting on the bank of the river with a line. I don't recall seeing any black persons until I was ten," he said.

As an adult, Stanley works for the Mennonite Church General Board. In a recent letter, he reflected on his experience of becoming aware of racism.

In late grade school I remember a time when some of the adults in my church made disapproving comments about the spending habits of the poor black and Hispanic people in an adjoining town. I recall that I was uncomfortable with the note of judgment in those comments.

In high school I began to realize that some of my language and metaphors were also racist. Then I noticed that judgment from the adult church was not reserved for black and Hispanic people alone. It could emerge fully developed in language that cut at anyone whose values or beliefs were different. This was very disturbing to me, but at the time I was too timid to speak to other people about what troubled me. I did, however, talk for hours to myself as I drove farm machinery in the fields. That was the beginning of my conversion from racism to Christianity.

Stanley came from a church community that did not talk about prejudice, let alone consider how they had been afflicted with the disease of racism. "Nigger fishing" was a common term. Stanley's sensitivity to the attitudes and language around him brought him to an understanding of his affliction. His story points to a fundamental way racism afflicts members of the dominant culture: it deprives us of the wonders of diversity.

I don't want to be set apart

Butch and Esther Gingerich live in Parnell, a small rural community in southeast Iowa, about twenty minutes from Iowa City. Butch is a hog and grain farmer. Esther is a clerk/receptionist at the educational placement office of the University of Iowa's College of Education. Together they've raised three children.

Butch and Esther usually don't have much reason to think about racism. Parnell is populated primarily by people of European descent. Butch and Esther are no exception. Esther can trace her family tree back ten generations to the mountains of Switzerland. So far she hasn't run into any of Butch's kinfolk. She says she won't be too surprised if she does.

Recently they had an opportunity to think more about race

prejudice and their privilege as white people. Even in a Mid-western rural community like Parnell, the impact of increasing ethnic diversity is being felt. Some of the assumptions they've carried about people of color and about themselves are no long-er helpful. They've begun asking questions about their parents' attitudes toward people of color, their first interaction with peo-ple of other ethnicities, and what it means to be white.

Butch remembers when he first discovered there was a dif-ference between white people and black people. Although he's not certain how old he was at the time, Butch remembers a fami-ly gathering at which one of his aunts received a present. She opened the box and found a dark-skinned doll. Everyone broke into uproarious laughter. Butch remembers wondering why ev-eryone found the gift so funny.

Esther attributes this sort of attitude to the fact that her par-ents and their peers rarely came in contact with people of other ethnicities. "When I heard our parents talk about a black person, it was as if the most important thing about them was their color," she commented. Esther observes that as her generation has come in more contact with people from other ethnicities, they have learned to see people as individuals.

When Butch was in elementary school, he would go to Uni-versity of Iowa basketball games. Many of the team members were African-American. "I thought they were great guys. They were my heroes," he said. They were also almost the only African-Americans he came in contact with.

Esther remembers one of the first times she came in contact with people of color. When she was in elementary school, each Sunday morning her family drove thirty miles to Sandtown Mennonite Church. The small mission church consisted of three Mennonite families who traveled in from surrounding commu-nities—as well as several local families, two of them black.

"My parents would invite different people home from church," she recalled, "including the black families. They treated them just like everyone else."

Both Butch and Esther have since had positive experiences relating across cultures. But they have been few and far between. They can list each one. A few friends in college. A friend Butch met through the church basketball league. A boarder they kept while she attended Iowa Mennonite High School. A few people Esther has met in the course of her work at University of Iowa .

Things are changing, however. They read of blatant racism and racial unrest in the not-so-distant cities of Waterloo and Dubuque. Esther discovers her own prejudice as she relates to Asian- and African-Americans at work. "Sometimes I feel a little superior. Deep down I know that's not true, but some of my feelings come out that way," she explains.

So they're pondering what it means to be white. One thing they've discovered is that white people often don't think about being white. "It's easy for us to ignore our color. I don't think people with other skin colors can do that," Esther surmises.

They speak of feeling guilty about being white as well. But they are satisfied with who they are. Referring to the time they hosted an African-American student from Chicago, Esther notes, "I don't want to be a person of color. When Sheila stayed with us, we discovered she was a beautiful person. Other people in the community looked at her as being black and didn't go any deeper. Even though she was involved in activities at school, she always felt like she was set apart. I don't want to be set apart."

How it got this way

Two things strike me about Stanley's story and the story of Butch and Esther. First, they can point to a specific experience through which they became aware of people of color. And in each instance, an innate discomfort with prejudice was apparent. Stanley was uncomfortable with remarks made by members of his church in reference to people of color. Butch couldn't understand why anyone would find a dark-skinned doll so humorous. Esther was glad her parents treated the African-American family from Sandtown Mennonite just like anyone else.

Other conversations I've had with members of the dominant culture about their first recollection of interaction with people of color reveal a similar innate discomfort with prejudice. Somewhere between childhood and adulthood, prejudices become ingrained. We are not born that way. We are taught.

A second commonality I notice is that no one asked, "Why have we been deprived of the wonders of diversity?"

Neither they nor members of their communities are unusual. The typical North American response to such questions is "because that's the way it is." Yet even a cursory examination of the history of retail practices provides an answer to these questions. Zoning board members and individual realty companies conformed to often unspoken practices that steered people of color in one direction and members of the dominant culture in another. People of color were either strongly discouraged or not allowed to live in white communities. Not yet a thing of the past, housing discrimination continues today.

Fortunately, rapidly shifting population demographics and some instances of active reformation of realty practices have begun to change the ethnic composition of the isolated communities that deprived Stanley, Butch, Esther, and many others of natural and frequent interaction with people of color. Other forces are working against the realization of multiethnic communities, however. Disappearance of public space in large urban centers, rapidly evolving telecommunications systems, and new transportation methods increasingly deny multiethnic interaction.

When housing patterns, church segregation, employment practices, and friendship choice keep us from entering equal relationships across cultural lines, white people are removed from the wonders of diversity. We become trapped in a lifestyle that encourages the lie of sameness. A lie that tells us it is better to be alike than different. A lie that repeats endlessly, "Same. Sweet, safe. Stick to the same. Same. Don't dare to be different. Same."

A four-cornered vision

The early church almost got caught up in this lie. Some Jews thought Gentile believers had to convert to Judaism before they could be baptized. They advocated sameness with great vigor.

Peter's four-cornered vision of a blanket filled with beasts and reptiles from all the earth, his interaction with the Roman centurion Cornelius, and his ensuing dialogue with early church leaders wrested that rigid conformity from the dogmatic hands that held it. His actions resulted in an opening of the gospel message to all peoples.

In Acts 10:34-35, Peter says, "I truly understand that God shows no partiality, but in every nation anyone who fears him and does what is right is acceptable to him." As easy as it may be for us to nod our heads to this ancient statement, I imagine the words sent shock waves through the early Christian community.

Perhaps people were afraid involvement with these unclean Gentiles would defile them. Perhaps rumors of Gentile plans to overthrow the Jewish leadership structure rippled through the community. Jewish society had long censured interaction with people outside their cultural and religious communities. Likely they feared they would lose everything.

Acts 10 makes clear that Peter's visit with Cornelius was outside the norm of acceptable behavior for an upstanding Jewish man. An angel of the Lord has to direct him to go with the three men sent by Cornelius. In later discussion with Cornelius, Peter makes a point of mentioning that "I came without objection" (Acts 10:29). Apparently other Jewish men of good standing would have objected; that Peter didn't deserved mention.

From our vantage point, we can see how much the early church gained by bringing these "unclean" Gentiles into community as full and equal partners. Few if any of us would call ourselves Christian today if not for the effort of Peter, Paul, and others. They responded to God's call to engage in the difficult, uncertain, often uncomfortable work of creating a new community in which "There is no longer Jew or Greek, there is no longer slave or free, there is no longer male and female; for all of you are one in Christ Jesus" (Gal. 3:28).

The early church decided to increase interaction with people different from themselves. No less a conscious decision is required of members of the dominant culture trapped in monocultural communities. Otherwise we continue to be sadly deprived of the richness of diversity.

A lie: white is right

A second way white people are afflicted with racism again

takes the form of a lie. Often we are taught to see our lives as normative, neutral, and ideal. As Peggy McIntosh has pointed out, this leads us to the assumption that the only way to benefit others is to make "them" more like "us."[1] This assumption afflicts members of the dominant culture in a variety of ways.

First of all it sets up a nearly impossible goal. Those we designate as "them" most often do not want to be like "us." In addition to certain privileges, white members of the middle-class experience recurring problems. Heart disease, rampant materialism, disintegration of the nuclear and extended family, high levels of stress, and high incidence of obesity all plague members of the white middle-class. Of course some of these problems are found in other ethnic groups as well, but they are particularly evident in dominant cultures. Being like "us" is not necessarily desirable.

Likewise this normative assumption adversely effects white self-esteem. Stanley Green has noted that perpetrators of racism are damaged because the "security of their selfhood is based on putting others down."[2] I suggest that mere assumptions of white as right or ideal also serve to damage self-esteem. We do not need to rely on skin color to establish confidence in who we are. Each of us is a precious creation simply because God made us.

When white people are taught to view our culture as normative, neutral, and ideal, we are diseased. Depth perception is denied us. We undervalue God's gloriously complex, rich, and superbly crafted creation. How can we say with the psalmist, "O Lord, how manifold are your works! In wisdom you have made them all; the earth is full of your creatures" (Ps. 104:24) if we place one culture above others?

Pounding on the door

Three years ago I was awakened in the middle of the night by someone pounding on our front door. I stumbled through the kitchen and peered out of the peephole to see who wanted in so desperately. There stood the same man who had come by earlier that evening to ask for money. Since we lived next door to a church that provided social services on certain days of the week, people would often come to the door for information about when the church would be open. A request for information was often followed by a request for money.

Those requests posed a dilemma that had by that time become far too commonplace. We did not feel good about giving money to people outside of a mutually accountable relationship. At the same time we wanted to respond compassionately to people in need, giving as freely to others as we had been given to. We've since become a bit more savvy in our assessment of requests, but we still get conned occasionally. I believe remaining open to God's call for compassion means we have to take risks. Sometimes we get ripped-off.

The man still standing in front of our door that night had come by earlier to ask for cab fare so he could take his sister to the hospital. We chose to help him out. When we gave him the money, he said he lived "just around the corner" and would repay us as soon as possible. I didn't think much of his assertion at the time, since similar promises regularly went unfulfilled, but there he was, at 1:00 a.m., insisting that he be allowed in so he could give my money back.

The loud pounding tipped me off that something was not right. Even in the haze of middle-of-the-night sleepiness, I recognized that it was unusual for someone to demand to repay a debt with such intensity at 1:00 a.m. After he refused to slip the money under the door because he said all he had was a twenty dollar bill, I told him he had better come back in the morning.

He said he needed to talk to me. When I again refused to let him in and broke off our increasingly bizarre conversation, he resumed pounding on the door. Finally he left.

I do not know why he pounded so hard. It could be he was going to demand more money. It could be he really wanted to pay me back. I'll never know.

When I finally got to sleep that night, my dreams were filled with pounding.

Victims of crime

It might seem that I have as much right as any other white person to believe that white people are regularly victimized by

African-Americans. If I were to believe media representations, word of mouth, and popular misperceptions, every African-American male under thirty is hell-bent on crime against white people. The man trying to get into our house was African-American. It would be easy to assume he was out to rob me.

He could have been, but as I said, I'll never know.

One way of examining my assumptions is to move from anecdotes to statistical evidence. It may then be possible to better answer the questions, "Who are the victims of crime and who are the perpetrators?" One common misperception is that white people bear a disproportionate brunt of crime. This is not true. As Brian Ogawa states, people of color, "particularly blacks and Hispanics, are victimized by violent crime relatively more often than other races."[3] Elliott Currie spells out these differences in the following passage from his book, *Confronting Crime*.

> Other things being equal, people in their late adolescence and early adulthood are far more likely to die by violence than infants and young children. But a black infant is more likely to be murdered in the United States than a white person of any age. Similarly, it's a truism that men—other things being equal—are more likely to meet death by violence than women. But other things are *not* equal. At every age until the late forties, a nonwhite woman faces a higher risk of death by homicide than a white man.[4]

Looking further, black men are nearly three times as likely as white men to be robbed, and cases of aggravated assault occur 1.5 times as often. Overall, forty-one out of every 1,000 black persons twelve years and over are victims of crimes. The rate is thirty-three per 1,000 for whites.[5]

Crime is always damaging, regardless of who perpetuates it and who is victimized. Although these statistics are important, I do not mean to suggest that crime visited on members of the dominant culture is deserved. Nor do I mean to suggest that people of color bring crime on themselves. I merely hope to show that white people are not the only ones crime harms.

Statistics also refute the popular misperception that white

people are most often victimized by people of color. According to the most recently available crime statistics, most white people (over 70 percent in the U.S.) are victimized by white people and most black people (over 80 percent) are victimized by black people.[6]

I will not attempt to examine thoroughly why crime occurs or how to prevent it. Others have studied these questions at length.[7] I will only add that incidents of personal violence are on the rise throughout all populations in North America.

We are all justifiably afraid of how commonplace violence has become. And so we members of the dominant culture cannot pretend that crime is only "our" problem. Crime affects all, regardless of race. We need to address crime as a common problem. Together we can look at the structural roots that bring crime about and develop appropriate strategies for addressing it.

Beyond violence

Moving beyond violence, I suggest that white people are afflicted with racism in a far more threatening way than personal incidents of crime. Certainly assault, robbery, burglary, vandalism, rape, and homicide are devastating; I am not trying to brush aside the tremendous trauma that comes with crime. However, on a systemic level, racism afflicts both white people and people of color by damaging the economy. As long-time community organizer Horace Seldon notes, "Racism, as one of the root causes of poverty, costs our nation huge amounts of money, measured in crime, unemployment and related social ills."[8]

If we overcome racism, if we find a way to open up housing, jobs, education, and access to capital so that people from every race and class have truly equal opportunity, we will all be better off. Less money will be lost to unemployment. Less money will be spent on crime enforcement. In the U.S., fewer dollars will go toward maintenance of one of the world's largest prison systems. Less human potential will be lost to the ravages of poverty, oppression, and inadequate education.

In the same way, working to undo racism requires that we look again at the true cost of crime in North America. Using examples from the U.S., which form of "looting" cost the most? Looting during the Los Angeles rebellions, 1991 street crime looting, or 1980s looting by the savings and loan industry? Looting during the L.A. rebellions cost $0.75 billion. Street crime looting during 1991 cost $14.9 billion. Savings and loan looting cost $450 billion.[9] We cannot ignore the fact that people of color are most often associated with the first two forms of crime, for which prosecution is much more harsh and swift. European-Americans were primarily responsible for the savings and loan scandal, but few of them will end up in jail.

Likewise, labor organizers have noted the way in which racism undercuts efforts to improve working conditions. When white workers are unable to unite with workers of color, it becomes much more difficult to advocate for livable wages and safe working conditions. There have been numerous incidents of management secretly paying people to foment racial dissent within the working place. Only as racism is overcome will such disruptive strategies prove ineffective.

It has been helpful for me to switch my thinking from "us versus them" to "all of us together." I have come to understand that one of the worst lies of racism is that white people have nothing to gain and everything to lose by actively working against racism. By refuting the argument that white people lose and people of color win when racism is dismantled, we recognize that white people are among the first to benefit in the new community, a place where racism is unknown.

Racism pounds on my door. But unlike the man who woke me in the middle of the night, this pounding has a far more legitimate purpose. It serves to awaken me to my own affliction. When I stumble to the door, I discover that the pounding comes from within. The longing for healing is already pounding inside my house, searching for a way out. I want to find healing. I believe we all do.

Peacocks, whales, and a white male writing

While preparing this material, I asked myself more than

once, "Why are you, a white male, writing about racism?" Others asked similar questions, expressing their concern that I may not be a credible source of information on racism. There are many reasons I kept on writing despite questions—longing that my children see a world in which white people are not afflicted with racism, belief that Christ calls us to a ministry of reconciliation across barriers of ethnicity and culture, and desire to help dismantle the barriers that have created oppression and meted out destruction upon people of color in this country.

The main reason I write about racism as a white male, however, is that I believe racism is a problem of white people. White people have created racism and we are afflicted with it. These afflictions do not take the same form as in racial ethnic communities, but they are harmful nonetheless. We have been deprived of the wonders of diversity. We have been led to believe the lie that white cultures somehow hold dominance over other cultures. We have been told the lie that we have nothing to gain and everything to lose by actively working against racism.

Racism afflicts white people in another way, one directly related to the experience of being white. During six years in New Orleans, I worked with many people of European descent who had not previously spent much time thinking about racism. Once they came in contact with a definition of racism that included an analysis of race prejudice and power, they sometimes responded in a troublesome manner.

Earlier I mentioned that white people are not bad simply because they are white. I say that again. I firmly believe we need an analysis of racism as race prejudice plus power. I also believe this definition is not an individual indictment of specific white people. The definition helps us understand the disease.

Yet I have heard white people say, "There's nothing I like about being white. I wish I were a person of color." How sad. Their statement reminds me of a song on one of my son Dylan's favorite tapes. RONNO (Ron Hiller), children's entertainer and educator, sings,

> Oh, I wish I were a Peacock, said the Whale
> So I had pretty feathers in my tail.

I'm sick of being gray
And swimming every day
I'd rather wear a crown
And strut myself around

The chorus replies, "We're all somebody, nobody else knows how to be. You couldn't be me if you wanted to, but you've got better things to do 'cause you're somebody special too and you're a gift to me and I'm a gift to you."[10]

Too simple? Perhaps. But these catchy lyrics make an important point. Whether whales, peacocks, or white people, we all have important gifts to offer. As we'll examine later, it is probably more helpful for members of the dominant culture to celebrate the gifts of our individual cultures rather than the far too amorphous white culture. Knowledge of our cultural roots and contemporary shifts and changes in those groupings provide us with solid grounding for interaction with other cultures. Each culture has gifts and weaknesses. Let's celebrate our strengths and work with our weaknesses.

Heroes dashed and discovered

I want to touch briefly on one more way white people are afflicted with racism. This affliction has to do with heroes.

When I was in sixth grade, I saved my allowance money to buy a book that revealed the origins of the superheroes. With few exceptions, each tale traced the development of an ordinary person to superhuman status. Those are the heroes I admire the most, people who come from ordinary backgrounds and go on to achieve remarkable ends. I've since graduated from the lexicon of comic strip superheroes who rely on violence to achieve dubious ends. Now I lift up heroes like Will D. Campbell, an Anabaptist novelist and earthy preacher, and Walter Wangerin, Jr., another novelist and poet.

We all need heroes and heroines, people to look up to, people we want to be like. Maybe we call them models, mentors, or guides, but we all have them.

For many years, North American educational systems taught

about historical heroes and heroines from only one perspective. I remember the white males of mythical stature who populated my textbooks: Christopher Columbus, George Washington, Benjamin Franklin. They could do no wrong.

I also remember the first time I read about Columbus. I mean really read about Columbus. It was during my sophomore year at college. We discussed the first chapter in Howard Zinn's book, *A People's History of the United States*. It told of the atrocities committed by the Spanish on the Arawak nation. War, slavery, torture, and introduction of disease virtually eliminated the Arawaks. Fifty years after Columbus' arrival in the New World, only two hundred Arawak adults remained. When he arrived, their estimated population ranged from three to eight million.

Due to the efforts of many people during the 500-year anniversary of Columbus' arrival in North America, this is old news. At the time I read Zinn, it was shattering news. A hero of my youth had died. Columbus, this stalwart figure, example of perseverance, holder of hope in times of utmost duress, helped to bring about the deliberate annihilation of millions of people.

I've since come to discover that George Washington owned slaves and Benjamin Franklin did not stick to his marriage vows with complete integrity. Part of discovering the underside of history takes place as we mature. I'm not sure I want my young children to know every shady secret of every historical leader. I am sure, however, that I want my children to understand that history is not made significant by the presence or absence of white males. I want them to read about people of color who were more than passive victims of historical forces. I want them to be presented with the history of other cultures before their supposed eclipse by the force of European expansion.[11]

I want my children to be taught about heroes and heroines they can be proud of. People like Bartolomé de Las Casas, a contemporary of Columbus who struggled to improve treatment of the Arawak nation; Henry Bibb, a leader of Canada's African-American population in the 1850s; and Sojourner Truth, an African-American woman who struggled against injustice in the days of U.S. slavery. Certainly these figures have their faults, but they did not participate in genocide or mass enslavement.

White people are afflicted by racism when taught about cultural heroes and heroines whose faults and collusion with oppressive systems are not portrayed. We are afflicted by racism when denied an education that includes varying perspectives from people of color.

We will learn much from study of the incredibly complex societies that rose and fell long before Columbus ever set foot on this continent. We will be better equipped to operate in a multicultural environment when we know how much "white society" has gained from the contributions of other cultures. We will be encouraged to stop the effects of racism when we discover again those heroes and heroines from history who struggled to bring about change in their own setting.

As white as snow

Returning again to the story of Naaman, we see a man who seeks healing because his "skin was white as snow" (interestingly a description of ill health, and thereby a startling reversal from usual connotations of white). He knows he is not healthy. He has recognized that he needs to spend time finding healing. So he sets out on a journey unaware of all that will be required of him.

One task members of the dominant culture need to take on before embarking on the journey toward personal and societal healing from racism is to find out the extent of our affliction. I have suggested a few ways in which we are afflicted with racism. There are many more.

Of course the list we develop will in no way resemble the list made up by members of ethnic groups outside the dominant norm. We may discover that our journey toward healing takes us along divergent paths. But by sharing the lists of our afflictions, we will at least know where the other is going and why. We can encourage each other to continue traveling, confident we are all moving toward a similar goal—the healing river.

In that river, no one has been deprived of appreciating the wonders of diversity. No one is led to believe the lie that white cultures somehow hold dominance over other cultures. No one is told the lie that we have nothing to gain and everything to lose by actively working against racism. No one's financial security is undermined by racism. Everyone cherishes his or her culture. Everyone holds up heroes and heroines who have struggled with integrity for justice.

Like Naaman, I and my people have been afflicted with a disease. Like Naaman, we have been given an invitation to wash in the river. Like Naaman, may we enter and find healing.

7

What Does It Mean to Be White?

That running white boy

In our neighborhood in New Orleans, one woman spent much of her day walking from street corner to street corner. Most often her hair flopped wildly as pink curlers threatened to spill out on to the sidewalk. She carried on a constant dialogue with someone only she could name. While out for my morning run, I occasionally heard references to myself. Amidst her confused, but imagery rich stream of invective, "that running white boy" slipped out almost too quiet to be heard.

Her assertion holds true. I am a running white boy. I run almost everyday. My skin has far less melanin than her's does. And having not yet reached thirty, I do not dodge too quickly when told I am a boy, especially when the teller is at least a decade older than I.

In those three words, she has referred to several central themes of my life story. The ability I have to run every morning indicates the nature of my work (I am desk-bound for the most part and desperately in need of regular exercise), my economic class (running is often a sport of the middle class), and my nutritional intake (it takes a solid chunk of calories to support my current running level of close to thirty miles a week).

She also notes I am a male. Job opportunities, relationships, familial roles, even basic human functions of procreation and waste elimination relate specifically to my gender.

The theme I want to spend the most time with here involves much more than my level of melanin. This confused streetwalking woman invokes a powerful term when she calls me white. So intricate and invisible that I do not have to think about it,[1] my whiteness is probably the foremost determiner of success or failure in the life ahead of me.

Before moving into further examination of the privilege underlying white skin, I want to tell the story of the rowdy class at Bishop Rummel.

The Rummel rowdies

One morning in 1992, I spoke to four classes of high school juniors at Archbishop Rummel High School in Metairie, Louisiana. Four days earlier rebellions had been sparked in Los Angeles by the acquittal of four police officers on trial for beating Rodney King. Rummel is located smack dab in the middle of the district that first elected former Ku Klux Klan grand dragon David Duke to the Louisiana House of Representatives. The school has earned a reputation for academic excellence over the years.

After telling a bit about myself, I opened my talk with the statement, "I am not going to speak about Rodney King, the KKK, or racial slurs." I limited my presentation to five ideas: 1. we have all been victims of prejudice; 2. the oppression of people of color is far greater than anyone who has not experienced that oppression can imagine; 3. people of European descent, beware of two things: we all carry stereotypes about people of color and we have been given tremendous privilege simply by having white skin; 4. we must cherish our cultures; and 5. to do nothing is to give our consent to the practice of racism.

The vast majority of the students were of European descent. Out of a class of 100 juniors, there were only three students of color. No African-Americans sat in any of the classes I spoke to.

The first class, the higher academic grouping, responded most belligerently to my presentation. Much of their discussion revolved around the "laziness of African-Americans," stories of "reverse" discrimination, and misconceptions about affirmative action. At one point one student exclaimed to class-wide approval, "Rodney King deserved every kick he got." Another student argued that white drug users were able to keep their lives together and provide for their families, unlike "the black drug users in the housing projects."

Even though I centered my discussion on white privilege and power, almost every question had to do with the condition of African-Americans. The students assumed people of color, not white people, were responsible for racism. Several students declared race had nothing to do with poverty or wealth. Several others stated with considerable conviction, "blacks can do whatever they want because of affirmative action."

I tried to stress the importance of critical thinking and understanding one's own culture. In response, a student from the first class asked if I would change my skin color if I had the chance.

"No," I responded.

Another student wanted to know if I liked white people.

"Yes, that's why I'm here today," I told him.

Still another asked whether I loved "the black people." He added under his breath that he didn't love them.

I was warned ahead of time about the third group, the rowdy class. "They respond with their hormones, not with their heads," warned their teacher, Mr. Dominique. I tried to prepare myself for lots of background noise and distraction. Halfway through my presentation, however, I began to wonder if Mr. Dominique had mixed up his class schedule. The students in front of me were listening much more attentively than had either of the two "smarter" classes before them.

I became aware that these were not people I would have chosen as friends in high school. The clean-nosed, college-bound overachievers I hung out with would have called these students "hoods." They sat in the back of the classroom, hung out by the convenience store after school, and partied hard on weekends— or so I was led to believe.

Yet this Rummel class of rowdies listened the most attentively and responded with the least belligerence of any group I spoke to. Two students from that rowdy class thanked me afterward for the presentation. One had grown up in an ethnically diverse neighborhood and said he agreed with what I said. Another was part Houma Indian. He told of how his grandfather had been denied access to the Louisiana educational system and had been forcibly removed from his land.

I can't help but ponder correlations between the content of my presentation and the attentiveness of the rowdy class. They understood the prejudice against them. Labels such as "rowdy," "hoods," even "stupid" had been applied to them too often. Out of that experience of prejudice they accepted the reality of oppression of people of color. They admitted their stereotypes and could identify the privilege given them simply by white skin. They had no trouble identifying with their own cultural roots.

This story demonstrates the great reluctance most white people have to examine the role of white skin privilege. And the story illustrates that those placed on the margins of society often more easily understand the privilege of white skin.

I do not want to suggest that students in the rowdy class were better people than students in the smart classes. Racism and white privilege are so pervasive in this society that they can be difficult to see. Even the students who so eagerly declared that Rodney King deserved every kick he got are not therefore bad. My guess is they were responding out of fear and strong racial stereotypes. I hope my time with them at least helped them to think again about what it means to be white.

A white mythology

What does it mean to be white? One way to start answering the question is to travel back to the colony of Virginia in 1691. Before then, "white" had never been used to describe members of a group. Skin color might have been labeled a particular shade of white, but that did not automatically place persons in a group.

According to research by Michael Washington, David Billings, and other members of the People's Institute for Survival and Beyond (PISB), "white" was first used in legal documents in Virginia in 1691 to describe an individual as a member of a group. Prior to that time, legal documents referred to Polish, German, Swiss, or English people. The use of "white" in that historical context coincided with efforts by members of the upper class to encourage lower class people of European descent to identify with them as white people. The wealthy elite was concerned that white members of the lower class might enter into the freedom struggle of people of color. Then as now, skin color was used to divide people who might otherwise come together to bring about change.[2]

As members of the PISB have helped me understand, "white" is a political, not a cultural term. It is entirely too bland, too nondescript, too conjectural to describe effectively the immense diversity of people of European descent in North America. Whiteness is a myth. We cannot gain a sense of history by tracing the roots of whiteness. I find no "white land" on the map.

I feel fortunate to have been brought up with a secure sense of my people, both as a child of Anabaptists and as a child of the Swiss and Germans. My parents have handed down to me many stories from their past. We gave our son the second name of Moses in honor of his great-great-grandfather, Moses Schmitt.

The very concept of race is a fickle construct. During a study trip to South Africa, Gerald Hudson was offered the status of an "honorary white" visa. Knowing that accepting that status would betray his identity as an African-American, he rejected the visa. Often he was refused service in restaurants, stores, and shopping malls. When they allowed him in, service personnel acted as if he were not there. If he had accepted the visa, he could have demanded service based on his "honorary white" visa.

Students of racial groupings remind us there is far more variety within a given racial group than between different racial groups.[3] Anthropologists developed the concept of distinct, quantifiable races. It is not a God-given construct.

Fewer and fewer peoples accept racial designations. As Andrew Hacker points out,

The nation's fastest-growing groups are rejecting racial designations. For example, we hardly ever hear allusions to the "yellow" or "Mongoloid" race, just as "Oriental" has all but disappeared. Chinese and Japanese and Koreans have chosen to emphasize their separate national identities rather than evoke a common heritage. Unfortunately the media have adopted the umbrella term "Asian," which tells us little about those under it, since they could equally well be Afghans or Laotians or Filipinos.[4]

Hacker goes on to observe that identifying individuals by the classic racial groupings connotes a "genetic determinism, often suggesting higher or lower locations on an evolutionary ladder." Because of these associations many peoples have chosen their own means of identification. Asians put their nationalities first, African-Americans identify with their dual culture, "while Hispanics prefer to stress the culture they created and sustain as a matter of choice."[5]

The privilege problem

Yet even as we begin to understand whiteness as a myth, we also become aware of the depth of our privilege as white people. How ironic that only in the process of moving away from a "white" classification do we come to understand how fundamentally that identification benefits us.

I first became aware of "white skin privilege" with the help of Barbara Jackson, president of the St. Thomas Residents Council in New Orleans. St. Thomas is a federal housing development which was about five blocks from our house. Barbara, an African-American, once said to me, "Suppose you and I walk into a bank together. If we said we wanted to make a deposit, the teller would assume you had come to help me. It would not matter that I had a million dollars in my pocket and you were penniless, the teller would assume you were in charge."

Peggy McIntosh lists privileges experienced by white people without their knowledge or consent. The list includes everything from freedom to choose housing location to seeing people like us in the media, and from locating a hairdresser to cut our hair to finding food from our cultural tradition in supermarkets.

My wife, Cheryl, and I spent much of the summer of 1991 speaking in Mennonite churches across the country on racism and white privilege. One of McIntosh's examples helped people understand the pervasive dynamic of white privilege. "White people can choose blemish cover or bandages in 'flesh' color and have them more or less match their skin."[6]

Until McIntosh drew my attention to the color of bandages, I never stopped to consider why first aid product manufacturers had chosen that specific color. Like me, they had not given thought or attention to what messages light colored bandages might send to potential buyers with darker skin colors.

As long as the assumptions behind such practices go unchallenged, people outside the dominant culture receive the message that their purchasing power, history, cultural contributions, or culinary preferences are not important. White people are led to believe the lie that their culture, history, and preferences are somehow chosen by God as better than others.

To my knowledge, God doesn't eat apples before mangoes, prefer blue jeans over saris, or place more historical significance on George Washington than Chief Seattle.

There are many other instances of white skin privilege. One blatant example comes to mind. I can call the police and be reasonably sure they will respond promptly to my call. African-American co-workers of mine who lived in the St. Thomas Housing Development reported lengthy lapses between their calls to the police and a response.

White privileges don't have to be blatant. They can be every bit as subtle as the color of a bandage. Here is my list of more subtle white skin privileges.

- I can walk through any popular tourist attraction without being held under constant surveillance by security personnel.
- I can cash a check without anyone questioning the validity of my identification.
- I can drive a new car home from the car dealership with-

out being stopped by the police because they suspect I stole it.

• I can explain that the library made a mistake without being accused of stealing a book the librarian claimed I did not return.

• I can easily find artists' depictions of Jesus, God, and other biblical figures that match my skin color and facial characteristics.

• I can attend a Mennonite church college or seminary and find a majority of professors who look like me, talk like me, and carry a similar set of assumptions about time, the value of academia, study, and relationships.

• I can call my landlord and ask to have an appliance repaired without being suspected of having broken it.

• I can shop at any department store in North America and find clothes that fit my cultural tradition.

• On television I can regularly see people like me in positions of authority and respect.

• I can shop for a new house without having to worry that the realtor may not show me all available houses in my price range

Every white person can write her or his own list of white privilege. I know of no better way for white people to continue the journey toward a truly multicultural community than to reflect on the privilege given them simply by having white skin.

One other privilege comes to mind. I can father children without anyone accusing me of doing so to increase my income. As service workers with MCC, our support plan is adjusted according to the size of our family. With the birth of our second child, our income increased accordingly. Additionally, all of Cheryl's medical expenses were paid by MCC.

Kiesha Jones (not her real name) is a friend of ours who lives in the St. Thomas Housing Development. She had two children roughly when we did. As a recipient of Aid for Families with Dependent Children, her support level increased with the births of her two youngest daughters. Yet our increase was substantially larger than hers. Because she is African-American and "on welfare" she becomes an undeserving target for the likes of David Duke. Not once in his bid for governor did Duke talk about "those religious volunteers having babies to increase their income." He did tell blatant lies about people like Kiesha.

Many of the privileges I have listed need to be equally shared. We all should be able to expect rapid response after calling 911. We all should be able to go to tourist attractions without being followed. We all should be able to conduct financial transactions without having our skin color influence other's opinion of our financial stability. The problem is not that white people have these privileges, but that people of color do not.

But not all white privileges are for sharing. Some are for throwing away. We are cheated of the wonders of diversity when academic faculty are from only one culture. We develop a skewed image of the world when we see mostly people like ourselves on television. We fool ourselves if we think any one of us should be able to buy a "flesh" colored bandage and have it match only his or her skin color. Insidiously woven into the fabric of our society, white privilege remains as ubiquitous as advertising, as invisible as oxygen.

A final privilege

More basic than any privilege mentioned so far is a remaining one which deserves consideration. White people simply do not have to deal with the harassment, intimidation, and oppression people of color must face—sometimes daily, sometimes weekly, but without fail.

White people don't have to put up with being followed in stores because of skin color.

White people don't have to deal with murmured racial slurs that take weeks to recover from.

And white people don't have to put up with the kind of obscene behavior exhibited in the following story.

On August 26, 1991, Orrin Ross was taking a ride with a friend. Orrin's friend and her young daughter, who rode in the back seat, are European-American. Orrin is African-American. They are old friends. Orrin was best man in her wedding.

Orrin had been wrapped up in a book he was reading while his friend and her daughter were arguing about radio stations. Then he noticed that a white car had been keeping up with them for a good distance. Orrin says,

> I looked over to see if it was someone either of us knew. It wasn't. The driver, who looked about nineteen had this expression on his face like, "What the h---'s going on here?"
>
> Before I could get my friend's attention and show her yet another bigoted person who thought we were obscene, they had pulled away.
>
> When we went to pass our recently acquired friends in the white Daytona, I expected them to do something but not what they actually did.
>
> The driver of the car mouthed the words, "I'm gonna kill you m-----f-----!" while his friend made a gun out of his hand and pretended to shoot me.[7]

I value the privilege of never having been faced with this sort of raw hate. I pray for courage, energy, and commitment to work for the day when Orrin will be given that privilege as well.

Back to the river

And what of old Naaman and wily Elisha? What does their story tell us now? If we as white people can put ourselves in Naaman's place again, several elements of the story jump out.

Naaman's skin disease did not keep him from performing well as military commander. Yet he was aware he needed healing. The servant girl, a most unlikely, almost powerless figure, pointed the way for him to find healing. He washed in the Jordan—a small, alien out-of-the-way river.[8]

As unglamorous, as uninviting, as difficult as washing not once but seven times in the Jordan may have been for Naaman, he was healed.

Could it be that we white people have to wash in our own Jordan? Might it be that our skin affliction is the disease of white skin privilege? Is it possible our journey toward healing may involve as uninviting a process as washing in a new understanding of the privilege given us?

Yet even as Naaman stood in that muddy little creek splashing himself all over, I am convinced that a steadily burning desire for healing filled him with determination, longing, and hope. Determination to see the process through. Longing for healing. Hope for a new beginning.

A break for feelings

I do not know the feelings that stir in you as you finish this chapter. You may be feeling anger, despair, confusion, hope, or guilt. Your feelings are valid. Discussing those feelings in a group setting may help identify how best to express them.

I have felt all the emotions listed above. I have felt angry at being kept uninformed for so long about such an important dynamic as my role in church and society. Despair has enveloped me at times when racism and white privilege seem too big to ever dismantle. I have felt confused when trying to sort through what is white privilege, what is accident, and what is irrelevant. And I have felt profound hope at discovering that white privilege need not keep me from destroying the dividing wall of hostility (Eph. 2:14) between Jew and Gentile; between white and black, brown, yellow, and red; between rich and poor.

Even knowing that white privilege is not the fault of any one individual, I still feel guilty at times over the benefits I have received. I've come to understand, however, that those feelings, valid that they are, lead me toward no constructive resolution of the problem of racism. Guilt freezes me, gums up the works, leads me to the false conclusion that to do anything I must change everything.

When I realize that sustained guilt only leaves me frustrated and empty, I turn toward longing and hope. The Jesus I know calls me to repentance, covers me in forgiveness, and pours out grace over all. As a white person, I need to ask forgiveness for remaining ignorant of my privileges. Having received forgiveness, I move toward a longing for further healing for myself and for the people of God. I am given new hope that we may yet see an end to racism in this country and church.

That we feel strong emotion when we discuss white privilege shows the important role race plays in our church and society. If we feel nothing but apathy, racism has won. Emotion is a sign of hope that we can change. When racism and the undergirding of white privilege that keep it in place are dead, we or our descendants will feel an even stronger emotion—joy.

Letting go and giving thanks

Perhaps we give up something in grappling with the privilege given us, but it is no more than what Christ asks of us in Luke 9:24—"Those who want to save their life will lose it, and those who lose their life for my sake will save it."

The first paradox we discovered earlier. Even as we reclaim cultural identities richer and fuller than white, we recognize the benefits we have received as white people. This second paradox comes as no surprise. Even as we lose our life (and perhaps some of our privilege), we save our life (and perhaps gain a whole new community).

I am thankful for the rowdy class at Bishop Rummel and the woman who stands on the street corner, pink curlers bobbing with the rhythm of her words. The rowdy class calls me to hope as they break out of their stereotype and identify with the oppression of others. The woman with pink curlers calls me to truth as she whispers my name, "running white boy." I whisper her's back, "she who calls out the truth in the midst of her pain." I pray for you sister. Pray for me, too.[9]

8

How Can We Celebrate Our Cultures?

In THIS CHAPTER we will use a broad definition of culture. Culture includes everything about us. Our thoughts, speech, beliefs, social forms, actions, physical appearance, artifacts, and knowledge make up our culture. We cannot exist without culture.[1]

This chapter has a twofold thrust. First, we all have cultures to celebrate. Whether we claim Swiss, Lakotan, Nigerian, Laotian, or Bolivian cultural roots, a combination of all five, or any of the thousands of cultures on this earth, our culture of origin impacts how we operate in the world. Both the culture we live in and our culture of origin give us much to celebrate.

Second, when cultures come together, the process of their interaction is invariably uncomfortable and rife with possibilities for misunderstanding. Yet the coming together of cultures can also lead to creative new ways of doing things, more flexible response to stressful situations, and a richer experience of what it means to be people of God.

Each cultural group—whether based on race, ethnicity, geography, class, or nationality—brings strengths and weaknesses to interaction with the world. In this chapter, I do not plan to set up charts of comparison between cultures. This only leads to comparing the best of one culture with the worst of another. Instead I hope to share a few more stories of how churches have come together across cultures, to look at scriptural accounts of the celebration of culture, and to return again to just what all of this has to do with white privilege in the context of racism.

Bakerview and Sandy Hill

Each church has its own culture, its own way of being in the world. Each congregation starts with the raw material of individual members' cultures and, over time, develops a culture of its own above and beyond the sum of its parts.

Two congregations from different parts of North America have come together across cultures. Though they struggle, they have not felt satisfied to let the gospel sit in the confines of monocultural congregations. The first story takes place in western Canada.

Bakerview Mennonite is a large Mennonite Brethren congregation of 700 members in Clearbrook, British Columbia. However, not size but three separate yet linked congregations meeting under one roof are what make Bakerview unique.

Some years ago a student from nearby Columbia Bible College approached Bakerview's senior pastor, Harry Heidebrecht, with a request for assistance in starting a Vietnamese congregation. With the support of the congregation, the student worked to build a church within a church. Today forty people attend a Vietnamese worship service every Sunday morning.

Not long after, a Hispanic couple met with Heidebrecht for prayer. Having felt God's spirit direct them, the couple started a Sunday school class conducted in Spanish. With assistance of a returning missionary from Latin America and the eventual leadership of a pastor who had fled El Salvador, the Sunday school class grew into a regular church service. Fifty people gather every Saturday evening for praise, worship, and fellowship.

Though the three congregations regularly meet in separate services, they come together for baptism, communion, and other special services. Heidebrecht exclaimed, "These experiences demonstrate our unity. The bilingual and trilingual services have been a real highlight of our life together."

This coming together has not been without frustration. After members of the one congregation had used the nursery, others felt it was not left in proper order. "My role was to act as an interpreter of Vietnamese culture to the larger congregation. We needed to understand a different, more permissive parenting style on the part of this group. They needed to understand our concern for order and maintenance of the property," Heidebrecht explained.

Heidebrecht added, "There's been growth on both sides. They've provided more supervision of children. We've grown to understand their parenting style better."

You don't need a huge infrastructure or separate meeting places to work at coming together across cultures. The experience of Sandy Hill Mennonite Church shows you can do a lot with a little.

Since the mid-1980s, Sandy Hill Mennonite Church (Coatesville, Pennsylvania) has become more diverse. In recent years, several African-American and bicultural couples have joined the predominantly European-American congregation. In 1991, some church members expressed interest in learning more about the culture of these new members of the congregation. At the invitation of church leadership, a committee was formed to plan an evening celebration of African-American culture.

The committee, made up of African-American and other interested members of the congregation, prepared a meal of greens, chicken, black-eyed peas, and sweet potato pie. To go along with the meal, they planned a program including a skit depicting a secret worship service among African-Americans held in bondage, poetry reading, spiritual singing, and a presentation on the contributions of African-American women.

A year later, the congregation invited the choir of a nearby African-American church to give a concert at Sandy Hill. After a carry-in meal and time of fellowship, the choir gave the concert.

One European-American member of Sandy Hill found the choir singing most meaningful. Dorothy Leatherman shared, "I regret having lived here in Coatesville for so many years without ever visiting an African-American church or hearing one of their choirs. It was a wonderful worship experience."

In addition to personal enrichment, the congregation reports that these celebrations have been a good way for members of the dominant culture to learn more about African-American culture, to develop friendships across cultures, and to see the gifts of all members put to use. Dorothy added, "Our congregation has been enriched by a diversity of race, culture, and background. God is making us into a family."

Both Sandy Hill and Bakerview have a long way to go before they are completely washed in the healing river. The realities of white privilege remain. Connecting across cultures won't end racism, but it is a start, a foretaste of the reconciled community.

When the wine overflowed

When I think of celebration in Scripture, many stories come to mind. The children of Israel rejoicing after crossing the Red Sea, King David dancing in the streets of Jerusalem, the prodigal son returning home, the vision in Revelations of the faithful gathered in the city of God.

But my favorite story of celebration is found in John 2:1-11. Jesus and his disciples are attending a wedding at Cana in Galilee. Jesus' mother is also there. The wedding has been in progress for awhile, probably several days. Most Jewish weddings at the time were seven days long. Jesus' mother comes up to tell him all the wine has been consumed. After expressing initial reluctance, Jesus changes six jars of water into wine.

The story has been carefully crafted. Numerous scholars and theologians have written at length concerning the theological nuances of this passage. For purposes of this chapter, I would like to limit my comments to a more cultural tenor.

I think it is significant that the first public sign of Jesus' ministry takes place in the midst of a celebration. And not just any celebration—but the celebration of a specific group of people, in a specific place, in a specific way.

As noted earlier, Galileans were frequently scorned in the

wider Jewish population. Jesus' first miracle takes place among these people, his own people, objects of ridicule that they are.

The author of John's Gospel takes pains to be certain his audience is aware this miracle took place not just in Galilee, but in Cana of Galilee. He mentions it twice. The most remarkable thing about Cana is that so little is known about it. Reference to it is made nowhere in the Old Testament and only once more in the New Testament. Contemporary historical accounts make almost no mention of it. Jesus' first miracle takes place in a no-account town of a no-account region.

Jesus also performed this first miracle in a specific way. The jars in which the water was turned to wine held over 120 gallons. Jesus blessed the bride and groom with abundance in the midst of derision. That abundance probably also came in the midst of poverty. Most families had to scrimp and save for years to get enough money to pay for the extravagance of a seven-day feast. The fact that no more wine was to be had may indicate the poverty they faced. Through Jesus' act, the host family is shown to be one which gives extravagantly and saves the best for last.

I like this story so much not because I want to encourage alcoholism. At that time wine was an important part of any celebration. If told today, the story might be about running out of desserts at a Germanic family reunion, then discovering that a larder holding only dry sacks of flour is overflowing with apple, shoo-fly, and blueberry pies. John doesn't tell the story to make a point about overindulgence in wine or food. John aims to show the power of Jesus sent to bring salvation to the world.

I like this story because, as it witnesses to Jesus' saving power, it also shows how important Jesus viewed celebration. Celebration was important enough to Jesus that he decided to change the water to wine even though his time had "not yet come." Jesus celebrates with his people in a culturally appropriate manner and gives glory to God.

Celebration is culture

I've spent time with this passage from John because I find it so rich in significance for the topic of celebration. I find several answers to the title question of this chapter, "How can we cele-brate our cultures?"

Any celebration that takes place among a people is not only a celebration of their culture, it *is* their culture. A celebration—whether for a wedding, funeral, other rite of passage, or just thanksgiving for the gift of life—will look quite different in the bayous of Louisiana than in a barrio of Los Angeles.

When those celebrations take place in the context of the church, we open many possibilities for enriching our collective experiences through the contribution of varied peoples. Such celebrations can bring us into relationship with people we would not otherwise have met.

Celebration is all the more authentic when it embraces the strengths and weaknesses of culture. Even though the members of that no-account town in northern Galilee may not have had much money, may not have pronounced their words as those in Jerusalem would have liked, and may have drunk too much wine too quickly, Jesus still entered and encouraged celebration. Jesus was no ascetic. He knew the place of celebration.

Celebration of our cultures is most authentic when it pushes at the edges of the expected. Whether saving the best for last or introducing new foods, celebration is most joyous when it respects the old, acknowledges its strengths and weaknesses, and adds new elements. The six stone jars are put to a new use while respecting their old function. And so the celebration continues.

What does this have to do with racism?

All this talk of celebration still leaves us with the difficult re-alities of white privilege and racism. What does celebration have to do with racism? Isn't it just a transparent avoidance maneuver to keep from doing the hard work of dealing with racism?

Certainly coming together across cultures is hard work with many pitfalls. This story from Lynn Herbach Cristini illustrates.

> While living in the Yukon Territory, Canada, I had an experi-ence I did not understand. It was a cold winter day with tem-peratures running around minus 40 degrees. It had been a long cold spell.

I was leaving the hospital with my baby daughter, in my four-wheel drive vehicle which was well-equipped for winter driving. We were warm and secure. As I left the grounds I noticed a lady standing on the doorstep holding a child close to her in an attempt to provide shelter from the bitter cold. The couple was Native American. It seemed unfair for us to be so secure and warm and for them to be so cold.

I pulled up in front of her, invited her to join us in my vehicle, and asked if she could let me know where she was going. She and her baby got in.

Except for her indicating where she wanted to be let off, we shared no conversation. She seemed reluctant to speak. We drove some two miles or so from the outskirts of the city into the center. I stopped for her to get out. Before she closed the door she looked in my direction and cursed me, "—you white lady!" She left me angry, hurt, and shocked by her insult.

Later I discussed the experience with a Native American friend. She suggested I should have asked the woman for something in return—even her watch if that was all she had. She explained that in the Native American culture, it is important to "trade" gifts.

This was a painful experience for Lynn and she has made herself vulnerable in the telling. Her story reminds us of the many misunderstandings that can take place across cultures. Our earlier examination of power and privilege also raises questions about history, assumptions, and structures. How do those systems give a white woman, a descendant of foreigners to the land, the privilege to own a four-wheeled drive vehicle while a Native American, descendant of the original inhabitants, stands by the roadside in freezing weather? The injustice in that difference in privilege explains in part the woman's angry retort.

Had Lynn and the woman been given the opportunity to celebrate together in a church or secular setting, their interaction might have been less mutually dissatisfying. The celebration would not have changed the inequity of their situations. But they could have gained a better understanding of how such gifts are exchanged and why it might be an insult to have to accept a ride without a chance for remuneration. Celebration across cultures is not a panacea for racism or white privilege, but it can open up doors to enhance understanding and increase interaction in a non-stressful environment.

It is probably most important for members of the dominant culture to seek out opportunities to celebrate in other cultural contexts. If we white people hope to increase diversity in our churches and church institutions, we must be willing to enter into unfamiliar turf where we may not be completely comfortable and celebrate with our sisters and brothers of other cultural traditions. Chapters nine and eleven give examples of how some churches have worked at this.

Celebration across cultures also reminds us that each cultural group has values and knowledge the others need. No one person or culture is whole without the others.[2] To put it another way, celebrating across cultures encourages us to change thought patterns from comparison (making one cultural aspect better or worse than another) to complementarity—where both are needed to make a whole.[3]

For example, for many years a melting pot myth warped popular perception of cross-cultural interaction in North America. According to this myth, a unique, almost magical property melted down cultural distinctions and produced a homogeneous people. The best of other cultures somehow stayed in the melting pot while the worst boiled away. We now know this myth to be a tragic untruth at best and a catastrophic falsehood at worst.

Images of salad, stew, mosaic, and stained-glass window provide much more healthy metaphors for describing the delicious and beautiful creations that spring from cross-cultural celebration. In these images, each culture maintains its own identity and integrity but adds to the overall flavor and beauty of the whole.

Now is the time to imagine new models of cultural interaction. In this way we escape the trap of tokenism, in which cultures are trundled out on certain days or weeks of the year for study and entertainment—but are not taken seriously as equally valid means of relating, worshiping, or communicating.

From the Crescent City

The final point I want to make about the importance of celebrating cultures comes out of our experience as Mennonite Central Committee service workers in New Orleans. Since 1980, when MCC first began work in the Crescent City, over thirty-five service workers have come to the city. The vast majority of them have come from Germanic, Swiss, and Russian backgrounds. Their work has established for MCC in New Orleans a tradition of excellence.

Local partners often told me that one thing they appreciated about MCC workers was the strong sense of culture and history they brought to their assignments. "Compared to several volunteer placement agencies," one partner remarked, "MCC brings people who value their culture and know who they are. They have a sense of their history."

This statement was neither a slam on non-Germanic/Swiss/Russian service groups nor an indictment of MCC service workers who come from other cultures. Instead, it was an affirmation of people who are grounded in their culture and are thus far better equipped to relate to other cultural groups than those who define their cultural identity as "white."

Of course, MCC and Mennonites have a lot of work to do in opening their structures to share power and decision-making across cultural lines. But that process of power sharing should not take place at the expense of undervaluing the benefits of a sense of history and peoplehood. The next step is to recognize that it is possible to celebrate and value individual cultures while learning and growing together at the same time.

During undoing racism training by the People's Institute for Survival and Beyond, we took time out from intense discussions to spend an evening celebrating cultures. One woman lit candles holding religious significance in her Jewish tradition. Another woman told a story about growing up in the rural South and the wonderful times her family had around the supper table. One man sang a rap song he had written. Still another participant told his story of personal transformation. At one time he had participated in violent demonstrations against people working to end segregation in the South. He now works to undo racism.

I told the story of an early Anabaptist, Dirk Willems, and his flight in the dead of winter only to turn and rescue one of his pursuers who had fallen through thin ice. I told how Dirk later died at the stake.

It felt good to share these stories and receive so many others. Many of the participants in that group have gone on to form the St. Thomas/Irish Channel Consortium, a group of social service agencies who work hard to reduce teenage pregnancy and address other needs in their community. Their alliance across lines of race, class, and religion is held together in part out of a profound respect for and continued sharing of cultures.

Groups like the St. Thomas/Irish Channel Consortium, Sandy Hill Mennonite Church, and Bakerview Mennonite Brethren Church show us it is possible to value our individual cultures, to come together as a diverse people of God, and to celebrate. Like those at the wedding in Cana, may we experience the gifts of abundance that celebration has to bring. May the wine flow like a river, a healing river, through the land.

9

What Does This Mean for the Church?

So FAR THE CHAPTERS OF THIS BOOK have led us to enter into the healing river. We have seen how race prejudice combined with power equals racism. We have learned about white privilege. We have celebrated cultures. Having learned these things and made a choice to work to change the realities of racism, we now find ourselves traveling in the river.

To put it another way, now that we've examined some of the realities of racism, white privilege, and culture, what are we to do? How do we, as Christ's body of believers, respond to racism in a racist society? What does this mean for the church?

I have set aside a separate chapter on the church because I am convinced lasting change is best brought about through the gathered body of believers. More than political movements, economic theory, or social analysis (although all three are essential), the church can be the source of change and redemption on both systemic and individual levels. Individuals can make a difference, but their impact is short-lived and temporary if not undergirded by a committed network of believers empowered by God's healing presence.

Though Christianity has been as much a perpetrator of racism as agent of racial reconciliation, I still look to the church as the place change can occur. In this chapter, I will lay the historical and theological groundwork for suggesting first steps the church can take to undo racism. Chapter eleven offers a more detailed listing of action ideas and examples of what others have done.

The stories that follow come from the North American Anabaptist tradition, a tradition as rich in witness to racial reconciliation as it is impoverished in action to change racist practice. I hope to present some of both—the best and the worst—as well as the in-between. Only by learning from the history of our church can we end racism in the present and beyond.

Mennonites and slavery

Any discussion of the history of Mennonite response to racism must take into account how Mennonites dealt with slavery in the earliest days of the U.S. On a positive note, Germantown, Pennsylvania, site of the first permanent Mennonite settlement in North America, was also the locale of the 1688 protest against slavery, "one of the earliest and clearest antislavery statements in American history."[1] The four men who signed the protest document were Quakers at the time, but three had been Mennonite back in Europe and one of the four rejoined the Mennonite church prior to his death.[2]

Their action is an exception in the Anabaptist tradition, however. As Theron Schlabach notes, while Mennonites rejected slavery on a personal level, "Mennonites did not crusade against slavery."[3] For example, the Virginia Mennonite conference explicitly forbade slave owning. If you had a slave, you were expelled from the church. However, if you tried to do something to stop the institution of slavery, such as working with the abolitionist movement, you were considered too political or worldly.

A few other incidents indicate the wide range of response between protest against, and noncooperation with, the institution of slavery. One Mennonite bought a slave only to give him his freedom after having a dream.[4] Another slept the night in an open field rather than be guest of a slave holder.[5] The son-in-law of a Mennonite bishop from Virginia denounced crusaders against slavery in a letter he wrote from Goshen, Indiana, in 1865. In the letter, he expressed relief that "our church and the Amish did not preach Negro in this county."[6]

Those of us in the Anabaptist tradition carry with us the legacy of those early struggles with slavery. I expect we have the most difficulty with the portion of that inheritance which makes us uncertain how to best bring about change. Do we focus on maintaining purity in the church? Or, do we take an active stance in the broader society?

We will only be able to answer such questions as we work out our faith in fear and trembling. Given Mennonite history, the answers will not come easily, but we cannot ignore the questions. We are changing too rapidly. We are too much in need of the river.

Church-planting among racial ethnic communities

European-Americans constitute the majority of the Mennonite Church in North America. According to the 1992 *Mennonite Yearbook,* 94 percent of participating members are defined as white. A different picture emerges, however, when congregations belonging to urban councils are examined. In those congregations, only 58 percent of members are white. Forty-two percent of members are African-American, Asian, Hispanic, or Native American.[7]

As we look to the future of a multicultural church and try to answer the many questions arising from rapid demographic change, we need to understand how things got this way. What influenced the development of current Mennonite diversity?

The answer, long and complex, involves varying emphases on evangelism, anthropological developments, economic influences, population shifts, immigration patterns, church structures, and the movement of the Holy Spirit throughout. Yet acknowledging this complexity and the hundreds of individuals who have given their energies to church growth in communities of color, it is still possible to make a few observations relating to our topic at hand.

Although there are many others, the four themes I have chosen to examine here are 1. the strong ethnic identity of early Mennonites in North America; 2. congregational growth as a function of indigenous leadership; and 3. the influence of cultural trappings.

First, Mennonites came to North America with a strong ethnic identity. As noted elsewhere in this book, Germanic, Swiss, and Russian cultural patterns were often superimposed over basic tenets of the faith. Worship order and other "civilized" matters of form were often confused with matters of substance.

Choosing only one example from a diverse and varied field of missionary endeavors, Rodolphe Petter, a Swiss-Mennonite missionary, provided an invaluable inroad to work among the Cheyenne by translating the New Testament into Cheyenne and writing a Cheyenne-English dictionary. However, even though he baptized hundreds of Cheyenne in Oklahoma and Montana, he continued to view them as little more than primitive children.

As Lois Barrett notes in her history of General Conference Mennonite Church Home Missions, when a fellow mission worker "introduced Cheyenne songs with traditional Cheyenne tunes rather than the western tunes which Petter used, Petter fairly exploded. . . ."[8] She adds, "No Cheyenne leaders were given full ordination as elders while Petter was alive."[9]

Second, we turn to leadership development. Study of racial ethnic churches indicates that when leaders of racial ethnic congregations and churchwide bodies reflect the ethnicity of those they represent, congregational growth and autonomy occur much more quickly than when members of the dominant culture lead. The history of Hispanic Mennonites in North America makes this particularly apparent.

The first Hispanic Mennonite services were held in September 1932. David Costillo was the first Hispanic pastor of that congregation. Fifty years later there were 50 Hispanic Mennonite congregation with 2,000 members.[10]

In comparison to African-American and Native American Mennonite congregations, Hispanic Mennonite churches have more quickly established a churchwide coordinating body. This is not because of more capable Hispanic leaders but because the legacies of slavery, segregation, and domination influenced rela- tionships between white Mennonite missionaries and African- American and Native American church members. As late as 1940, the Virginia conference of the Mennonite Church ap- proved a statement that encouraged racial segregation, even to the point of recommending individual cups at communion for "the colored and those who are regular workers among them."[11]

Third, when the gospel message is presented with a mini- mum of cultural trappings, greater receptivity occurs. For exam- ple, one could question how appropriate it was for the pastor of Brentwood Mennonite Church to encourage African-American Mennonite leader James Lark to don the plain coat (at the time a symbol of biblical simplicity worn by most Mennonite men) on joining the congregation. Lark wore plain clothes but took the plain coat off when he "went downtown to do business."[12]

As we look for a healthier interplay of Mennonite ethnic and racial groups in the future, three areas will need attention.

> **Church structures**. How can we change church structures truly to include the growing number of racial ethnic members?
>
> **Resource distribution**. How can we address white privilege and more equitably distribute resources across the church?
>
> **Faith's form and substance**. How can we discern what of the Anabaptist understanding of the gospel is form (cultural variety) and what is substance (common faith)?

A tour through the South

We can no longer afford the delusion that cities in the U.S. South, and churches located there, hold primary responsibility for dealing with racism. Having said that, there is still much to be learned from churches in the South. While they may have been unjustly given entire responsibility for racism, many churches have faced racism head on. Some have done so more openly and creatively than others, but almost none have completely ignored the need for racial reconciliation. If nothing else, churches in the

South are on a journey toward the river. However long and circuitous that journey may be, it remains in progress.

In the summer of 1963, Guy F. Hershberger was commissioned by the MCC Peace Section (with support of the Peace Committee of the Lancaster Mennonite Conference) to visit Mennonite churches in the South for three weeks. He gathered information from the churches and helped interpret convictions of the larger church regarding race relations. From July 26—August 16, he and his wife, Clara, visited seventeen different cities in Virginia, North Carolina, Georgia, Florida, Alabama, Mississippi, Arkansas, and Missouri. Their visits brought them in contact with representatives of over forty congregations.

At each stop, meetings were held to discuss racial reconciliation. Thirty years later, the comments recorded in Guy's report reflect the message and mood of the times. Two main concerns recur throughout. First, churches should be open to people of all races. Second, church members should change attitudes about African-Americans.

Clara and Guy were faced with overt racism, evidenced in statements like, "You're just trying to bring niggers into our church." They also encountered corrupt theology, evidenced in the assertion that "if a Negro was truly Christian and knew his presence in a white church would offend even a small percent of the congregation, out of Christian concern not to offend he would not attend." Many of the churches did not want to open their doors to African-Americans for fear non-Christian white people would never be reached. Others feared desegregation was a communist plot to overthrow "Bible-believing Christians."

While Guy expressed deep concern over the heavy prejudice he encountered in some of the white churches, he was basically optimistic that the "racial revolution" would overcome these setbacks and bring about a new community. His recommendations included implementing a South-wide inter-Mennonite conference on race relations, increasing education on churchwide statements, encouraging industrial development among racial ethnic communities, and increasing church organization personnel in areas of racial tension.

After reading over his report, I was discouraged to realize

that, with minor changes, his report could have been written in the 1990s. A majority of the churches he visited remain segregated—if no longer in principle, still in practice. While he probably would not encounter as much overt racism, the vast majority of church leadership and resources throughout the Mennonite church remain in white hands.

Of the 2,012 ministers in the Mennonite Church of North America, seventeen are Asian; forty-four, African-American; seventy-six, Hispanic; two, Native American. While those figures parallel the number of people of color belonging to Mennonite Church conferences (about 7 percent), they fall far behind the country as a whole (people of color constitute nearly a fourth of the U.S. population).

Much has changed in the last thirty years. But Vincent Harding's piercing analysis of Mennonite responses to racism remains as appropriate now as then. Harding, now on the faculty of Iliff School of Theology (Denver, Colo.), was quoted by Hershberger as saying, "Not enough effort has been made to . . . find many 'natural occasions' for [coming together across racial lines] because we have been living in an unnatural (segregated) situation so long that real effort will be required to create a natural situation once more."

Harding continued, "The question . . . is not whether there will be opposition [to working to dismantle racism], but rather what is right. When we say we must be careful about our influence, the question really is whether we are concerned for our influence or our affluence. *It is rather when we are too much concerned for our affluence that we really lose our influence for good* [emphasis added]."[13]

The military and the Mennonites

Vincent's remarks are made all the more prophetic when placed next to a story about Mennonites in De Ridder, Louisiana. At the time of Guy Hershberger's arrival, he reported that the "De Ridder Mennonites seem to have a good attitude toward the colored people although many do not employ them," and that several members of the congregation used derogatory terms when referring to their African-American neighbors. A few changes had begun to take place, such as desegregation of lunch breaks on Mennonite carpenter crews and an integrated funeral held for a white member of the Mennonite church. But many businesses in De Ridder remained "whites-only."

They might have continued as segregated businesses for a long time. As it turned out, the military did far more to end that form of racism than did the Mennonites. The U.S. Army camp at Fort Polk was only fifteen miles from De Ridder. When the Army declared segregated business establishments off limits for all camp personnel, changes immediately took place. Given the economic impact of the camp on the area, this policy carried considerable influence. Hershberger noted, "the son of a Mennonite family . . . had a business establishment with a 'white only' sign on display, but which was promptly removed following an ultimatum or a rebuke from a Fort Polk official."[14]

We can only wonder what effect the Mennonites of the De Ridder community could have had if they had only done business with those who did not practice racial discrimination. Were they more concerned about their influence or their affluence?

Of course we cannot be too hard on a group of people living thirty years ago. I include this story to demonstrate the power of money, not to degrade the power of the church. Yet I have to wonder why an institution like the military can make such a dramatic difference in a community. Should not an institution like the church make even more impact?

The church can make wonderful, theologically sound statements on racial reconciliation for years on end. Such words, important as they are, will not be remembered thirty years down the road; the actions taken by people of faith will.

A brief discussion of faith and works

Right attitudes are important, but actions bring about change. The director of a leading undoing racism training group told me, "You're only undoing racism if you're working to undo racism. You're only antiracist if you're doing something against racism." Seems obvious in a way. Also a bit threatening.

I suspect his statement leads to conclusions that may set some grace-conscious theologians on edge. Are we redeemed because we believe or because we act? It's the eternal tension between faith and works. In the context of racism, I suspect we white people have a lot more work to do on the side of works than faith.

For purposes of this book, I have assumed that once people of faith see how racism manifests itself in contemporary settings, they will recognize its inherent evil. This will lead to longing for racial reconciliation. In a sense, I am assuming I do not need to encourage people in the belief that racism is wrong.

The Scriptures and stories we have looked at make clear we are called to be a reconciled community. The problem is not so much the presence of heterodoxy (wrong belief) as the absence of orthopraxis (right action). In other words, we know what we want to do but don't do it.

Before moving to a brief discussion of a paradigm for multicultural mission and further suggestions for the church's response to racism, let's look at two stories of how other churches have responded to the reality of racism and white privilege.

In Kansas, the unexpected

In the midst of Kansas, far from inner-city racial rebellions or histories of Southern segregation, a small Mennonite church ventures outside of its cultural boundaries to do the unexpected.

Salina, Kansas, counts no more than 42,300 people on its roles. Of those, approximately 3.5 percent are African-Americans. Salina Mennonite Church worships in the midst of this predominantly Germanic community. Members also work at dismantling racism.

Dismantling racism? In Kansas? Certainly not there. Salina is a long way from Montgomery, Alabama, or Jackson, Mississippi.

"Not so," said Salina Mennonite copastor Christine Juhnke. "We discovered that racial tensions were escalating." Along with several other churches and civic groups in the city, Salina Mennonite has tried to implement God's call to dismantle racism.

Salina Mennonite deliberately set out to build relationships across cultures in a church context. "There were already strong friendships among our congregations," Christine noted, referring to Baptist, Independent, and United Methodist congregations with African-American leadership.

Christine helped build connections by inviting the pastor of a Baptist congregation to help plan a community worship service as part of an ecumenical ministries conference. Both African-American and white leaders planned and led the worship service, a highlight for many who attended the conference. Christine stressed the importance of such worship times, "Worship is a place where we're on equal ground. In worship we are able to recognize our commonality."

An Independent congregation joined Salina Mennonite for Sunday morning worship services as well. The Independent congregation's pastor preached. After his sermon, members from both congregations divided into three large circles to talk about their commonality in Christ, common concerns for their community, and other shared values and experiences.

When asked what has brought members of her church the most joy as they've worked across cultures, Christine responded, "Making new friendships and building bridges across racial and economic barriers."

There have also been frustrations. "Busy schedules limit the extent to which we involve ourselves. There are so many things to do in the church, so many people and causes to care about. Sometimes we get frustrated with people's attitudes. Complacency in the face of racism disturbs us. But we also recognize that racism is subtle and pervasive; we as white people have limits to our understanding," Christine added.

In spite of those frustrations, they move forward. In addition to ongoing relationships with the other congregations, the outreach committee of Salina Mennonite is attempting to network with other groups in the community around undoing racism. They are also working within their church to become more conscious of their attitudes and to build an awareness of the power and privilege given to white people in North America.

Building Community

Community Mennonite Church is an integrated congregation in Markham, Illinois. Average worship attendance is sixty-
five. Approximately half are African-American and half people
of European descent. Most church committees are proportion-
ately representative of the congregation. Currently there are
three Anglos and one African-American on the Board of Elders.

David Ewert accepted a full-time pastorate at Community
Mennonite Church in 1986. Soon after he entered this position,
he and the church council began to think more about what it
meant for a church to be not just integrated but truly reconciled.
As a member of the dominant culture, David believed such reconciliation needed to be expressed at the leadership level.

The congregation began to process these ideas along with
Ewert. In 1989, the congregation affirmed Ewert's decision to cut
back to part-time so the congregation could add a person of col-
or in a ministry position.

Les Tolbert was hired. For two and a half years, Les and David worked together on the team. During that time, David faced
the challenge of learning to relinquish control. "At times it was
difficult to allow Les to lead, especially when he was doing
things in ways that made me feel uncomfortable," he confessed.

As Les and David continued to work together, they struggled
to find ways to help such a diverse congregation worship. Not
only did they have to deal with differing expectations of cross-
cultural interaction, they also had to take into account diversity
of beliefs. "Theologically we span the spectrum from radical
'peace and justice types' to evangelical charismatic to traditional
Christian," he explained.

Over the years, the congregation has chosen a participatory
form of worship. David mused, "To people expecting spit and
polish, our services may seem sloppy. But we have chosen to
allow many individuals to use their gifts."

Both pastors had to fit their preaching to the needs of the
congregation. At one point, an African-American church elder
told David, "Be who you are. Don't try to be like the other pastor.
Be who you are."

"This was freeing for me," David recalled. "Although I have

learned to rely less on notes when delivering a sermon, I don't feel pressure to act like someone I'm not when in front of the congregation."

As of this writing, Les has returned to his home community to further his schooling, but the congregation is not ready to go back to a single white leader. David said, "I've wondered about working myself out of a job to give a predominant role to black leadership." Although lay leadership is shared across ethnic lines, an African-American has never been congregational chair or treasurer. "It's unsettling to think about, but we're looking at our model of leadership and asking questions about money, positions of power, and who sets the agenda," David added.

"We never get over dealing with prejudice. We can't stop paying attention to black and white issues. The dynamics of inter-racial relations are always there," David concluded.

Yet in spite of areas in need of attention, Community Mennonite has seen realized the promise of Ephesians 2:14: "For he is our peace; in his flesh he has made both groups into one and has broken down the dividing wall, that is, the hostility between us."

Models for change

So far in this chapter, we have examined Mennonite history regarding slavery, church growth in racial ethnic communities, and a response to the movement for racial justice in the South. We have seen the good of an entire body of people refusing to participate in the institution of slavery. We have seen the bad of Christian ministers advocating racial separation. And we have seen the in-between as church growth efforts brought the good news mixed with sometimes restrictive cultural practice.

The stories of Salina and Community Mennonite churches give us examples of how contemporary Anabaptists have answered God's call to work at racial reconciliation. What do these contemporary stories and this history teach us?

Must every Mennonite businessperson refuse to do business with anyone who engages in racist practices? Should we set aside all church outreach money for work in racial ethnic communities? Does every full-time white pastor need to become part time to make room for multiethnic leadership?

Even if I set out a detailed blueprint for answering these questions, I expect few would adhere to the recommendations. None of us want to be told how we must respond to the reality of racism. The response will be different in each setting.

We can, however, present a model for ministry across cultures. The model will not determine the specifics of how we respond to racism and white privilege in our context, but it can point us in a common direction.

In their workshop, "Developing Harmony Through Diversity," Brent Foster, Noel Santiago, and Carlos Romero help congregations examine their models for ministry. In the workbook that accompanies their presentation, they examine two models of multicultural ministry.

Any given model is always based on a set of often unexamined cultural assumptions. Those assumptions form the gridwork holding congregational ministries in place. The purpose in examining those structures is not to suggest structures are bad for being structures. As Brent, Carlos, and Noel note, "Structures are necessary and an integral part of all cultures."[15] Rather, the examination of structures helps highlight how any given model impacts other cultural groups.

The first model, Figure 9-1, is entitled, "A Colonialistic Multicultural Ministry Model." In this model, the dominant culture plans, evaluates, and coordinates any given event. Only after plans have been made are racial/ethnic groups invited to respond.

In the course of this response, several dynamics take place. Only one person responds as a representative of the entire race or ethnic group; those who come into the dominant culture circle tend to act less culturally authentic within the dominant culture circle than in their own; little or no relationships exist between the different racial/ethnic groups outside the dominant culture sphere; and the relationship among the diverse racial/ethnic groups within the dominant culture circle is characterized primarily by competition for attention and resources.

The outcome of this model is a caricature that does not empower the racial/ethic groups or meet their particular needs.

Brent, Noel, and Carlos go on to list several other characteristics of this model—it is confrontational, applies standardized dominant culture values to all involved, has little or no flexibility, is control oriented, seeks its own preservation, and has a decision or product as its primary goal.[16]

The second model Figure 9-2, is entitled "An Authentic Multicultural Ministry Model." This model is vastly different from the first in one fundamental way—how power is distributed. In this model, power to plan, coordinate, and evaluate is shared in a common arena. Instead of decision-making being channeled through dominant culture channels, the decisions are made in cross-cultural concert.

Regardless of how a congregation develops a more authentic multicultural ministry, the essential question is who has the power. If we ignore that question in the Christian community, we can never with integrity ask the question of the larger society.

One thing I value in the Mennonite church is healthy suspicion of hierarchy. A long tradition of the "priesthood of all believers" will serve us well as we shift to more authentic models of multicultural ministry.

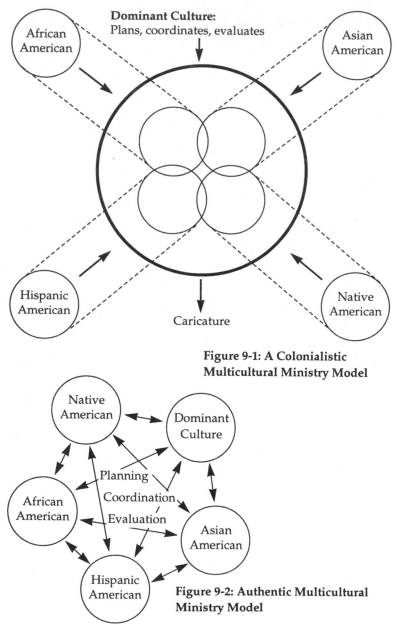

Figure 9-1: A Colonialistic Multicultural Ministry Model

Figure 9-2: Authentic Multicultural Ministry Model

And here is the hope

As we come to the end of this chapter, I am reminded of a statement Hubert Brown makes in *Black and Mennonite*. Brown writes, "The believer's church is Christ's church, and because it is Christ's church it can never be an ethnic fellowship, a private club of restricted membership."[17] That statement clearly defines the current challenge for the Mennonite church.

Mennonites of European descent have brought strengths to the church. The problem is not their ethnic identity, but that this identity has partially defined what it means to be a Mennonite.

The church is much more than any one ethnic group. As Brent Foster, former evangelism and church development consultant with Mennonite Board of Missions, has said, "Ethnic groups have to have an identity apart from the church before they can truly have an identity within the denomination."[18] Likewise, José Ortiz, former director of Hispanic Ministries at Goshen College, has noted, "Mennonites cherish and protect their right to be themselves. We should ask for nothing less."[19]

Before we as a church can realize full racial reconciliation, all members will need to find their own sense of place and peoplehood. This may seem like movement away from inclusion, but it is the only way to avoid falling into the traps of paternalism and cultural subjugation that have too often characterized racial ethnic involvement in the Mennonite Church.

As imperfect as the church may be, I am confident it can change and bring about change. That conviction comes from seeing churches that have confronted racism and struggled with it. In facing racism, they have confronted death. That confrontation itself is hope embodied. William Stringfellow once wrote that "hope is known only in the midst of coping with death. Any so-called hope is delusory and false without or apart from the confrontation with the power of death. . . . Resistance to death *is* the only way to live humanly in the midst of the Fall."[20]

May we be given hope and strength to resist death, to confront racism, and to enter the healing river again and again.

10

What About Affirmative Action?

UP TO THIS POINT we have examined racism primarily in the context of the church. I have tried to hold up a vision of a gathered body of believers working together to create a new community that struggles with white privilege, celebrates cultures, and actively works to dismantle racism. I believe in that vision and hope to be part of bringing it about.

Racism does not exist solely in the church, however. It is also heavily manifest in the workplace. And it is there, where dollars meet dimes, that the test of our commitment to dismantling racism becomes most strenuous. I have asked myself more than once, "What does emphasis on increasing diversity in the workplace mean for someone like me, a white male? Can I support affirmative action if it means I will have less chance to do the work I feel called to do? If I advocate for an end to racism, don't I risk moving from racist oppressor to victim of reverse racism?"

I am not proud of those questions. But I have asked them. And my guess is that I am not alone. In both good and bad economic times, everyone is concerned about finding adequate employment. Those concerns are heightened when demographic change is thrown in the mix. Demographers anticipate that shortly after the year 2000, African-Americans, Hispanics, and Asian-Americans will constitute nearly half the U.S. work force.[1] How can the church respond to these changes without discounting the fears of dominant culture members or stepping back from assertively working at bringing an end to racism?

In this chapter I hope to propose one way to answer that question. By examining closely some of the most commonly asked questions about affirmative action, I think we white people can come to see that affirmative action programs will benefit us as much as anyone else. Some difficult and painful decisions will need to be made along the way. But there is a history of far greater pain and outright oppression that calls us to make those hard decisions now as we move toward a more inclusive future.

With the exception of an opening story, this chapter will depart somewhat from past chapters to follow a question and answer format. Since questions about "reverse racism" and affirmative action seem such a stumbling block for so many members of the dominant culture, I think those of us committed to ending racism need to be prepared to dialogue about as many of those questions as possible.[2]

Ain't I a man?

A recent houseguest told us a story he said was about "reverse racism." Halfway through his morning magazine delivery route, Joe stopped by a convenience store for coffee. On the way to fill up his mug, another customer stepped in front of Joe. Seeing what had happened, several of the other customer's friends derided him for stepping in front of Joe. The man responded, "Ain't I a man? Can't I get a cup of coffee?"

Feeling uncomfortable, Joe waited until the customer was finished, filled his mug, and quickly left. Joe is a European-American. The other customer was African-American.

As Joe told us of the incident, I found myself wanting to respond, "How is this racism? What is reverse about it?" Given the constant oppression and indignities faced by people of color in North America, I have a hard time seeing Joe's experience as an example of any kind of racism. As we have explored, racism is more than simple acts of discourtesy. It also involves power and privilege, forces deeply ingrained in our society.

But I understand Joe's discomfort. I even understand why he sees his story as an example of reverse racism. In his view, affirmative action encourages people of color to cut in front of white people who are moving toward what legitimately belongs to them. Unfortunately, a majority of the dominant culture population in North America view affirmative action in much the same way—"Those people butt in line instead of waiting their turn."

As we will later see, that metaphor is far from accurate. Affirmative action is much more a process of opening previously closed doors than of butting in line at the coffee stand.

In this chapter, I will show how affirmative action programs open doors. While not the final or only solution to racism, affirmative action programs can help us make good our commitment to moving toward the healing river.

Question #1: Do affirmative action programs really work?

Yes. Even if we limit the goal of affirmative action to a simple examination of increasing diversity in the workplace, affirmative action programs have been quite successful. When enacted with the vigor and commitment necessary to make words on paper a reality, affirmative action increases diversity in the workplace.

For example, statistician Theodore Cross has written that

> during the late 1970s, Census figures show that black men in managerial positions dramatically increased from 2.8 to 6.9 percent of the total, a 146 percent increase. . . . Gains in these fields were much less dramatic during the 1960s (1.6 percent to 2.8 percent), a period usually characterized as the "pre-affirmative action era."[3]

Furthermore, in a study of 77,098 businesses from 1974 to 1980, Cross discovered that racial ethnic employment grew by 20.1 percent in businesses required to adhere to affirmative action practices, but only by 12.3 percent in other businesses.[4]

However, it is important to note here the argument regarding affirmative action made by Stephen L. Carter and others. They maintain that programs of racial preference do not help those who need it most—people of color on the lowest end of the economic scale. Likewise they argue that, if affirmative action is meant to redress wrongs of the past, it exacts no cost from those who as a group have most actively perpetuated racist practices—wealthy white males.[5]

This argument deserves attention, but I do not believe it negates the worth of affirmative action programs on the whole. Rather, the argument merely points to the fact that we need to choose from a broad range of programs and actions to address racism. Affirmative action has limits, but it has made and continues to make important improvements.

Question #2: So aren't things better now?

I wish I could say yes. However, due to deliberate undercutting by the courts and federal government during the 1980s and 1990s, those early gains have not continued at their initial pace.

Even in the Equal Employment Opportunity Commission (EEOC), the federal body given the task of enforcing civil rights legislation, affirmative action has been under attack. During supreme court justice Clarence Thomas' tenure as EEOC director (1981-1986), the number of discrimination suits filed were reduced by 25 percent and the number settled in favor of the complainant fell from 32 percent to just under 15 percent.[6]

We need to recognize that despite the gains of affirmative action up to the early 1980s, people of color continue to be oppressed. We have examined this oppression at length elsewhere, but it is worthwhile repeating a few statistics—

• white businesses control 99.7 percent of the Gross National Product;

• black professionals and managers are twice as likely to be jobless as their white counterparts;

• blacks with comparable training and experience as whites earn only 55 percent as much as whites.

Quoting again from Wise,
The bottom line is that discrimination against blacks is
pervasive, and systematic. Recently, the EEOC revealed that
temporary agencies were engaging in a "national crime wave
of discrimination" by filing slots for whites only.
Furthermore, the Urban Institute reports that 67 percent of
all blacks face discrimination when attempting to purchase a
home, and 75 percent are discriminated against when
attempting to rent. As recently as 1987, a court had to order
one Louisiana business to finally tear down its segregated
rest rooms![7]

While I have limited my statistics to a comparison of African-
Americans and European-Americans, similar dichotomies are
present for all people of color in North America.

The situation has not significantly improved. We have not
yet arrived. And where there has been improvement, it is pre-
carious. Affirmative action is one attempt to address wrongs
centuries old. We have tried affirmative action for less than thirty
years. We have a long way to go.

Question #3: Doesn't affirmative action demean people of color?

Behind this question is the assumption that affirmative action is paternalistic. The argument is that since affirmative action
is basically a handout to people of color, they are somehow being demeaned. In essence, this line of reasoning suggests that affirmative action is harming people of color by not requiring
them to "pull themselves up by their bootstraps."

Assume for a moment that affirmative action is a handout. If
so, why do we never hear a similar argument used to deny benefits to veterans of the armed forces? Veterans receive preferen-
tial treatment under many federal guidelines. Often guidelines
for hiring veterans give preference far more assertively than do
guidelines for hiring members of racial ethnic communities.

Also, no one bemoans land grants given to early North
American immigrants. Setting aside the fact that this land was

not theirs to give away, I've never read a passage in a history book that derides the U.S. government for handing out land parcels to these almost exclusively European immigrants.

Other sorts of federally mandated "charity" abound—tax breaks, capital gains cuts, and numerous loopholes for the wealthy. These are never labeled paternalistic either.

Even without these discrepancies, the fact remains that affirmative action is not a handout. Affirmative action is compensation. It attempts to redress the injuries inflicted on a group of people for centuries. As such, about the only way affirmative action demeans people of color is when employers act as if people of color will never be as qualified as whites. Those who hold such an attitude are bound to hire persons of color only for the most menial positions. Affirmative action is not the problem; blatantly racist attitudes of those who suggest that one race is genetically inferior to another are the problem.

Anthropologist Eloise Hiebert Meneses, faculty member of Eastern College, notes that 150 years of attempts to classify people by races have failed. "No single trait or cluster of traits," says Meneses, "will neatly separate one group from another."[8] If nothing else, affirmative action programs remind us it is precisely because no ethnic group has a genetic advantage over another that we need to level the playing field for those who have been kept from realizing their full potential by the dynamics of power and privilege.

Question #4: Who is qualified?

Fundamental to affirmative action is qualification or merit. One type of affirmative action program operates on the principle that when two applicants are equally qualified for a position, the racial ethnic applicant should get the job. A question that arises from this approach is, "Who really is qualified for any given position and how can this be determined?"

Prior to the enactment of affirmative action legislation, many businesses used certification tests that had little or nothing to do with job performance. While this practice continues in some institutions which are not required to meet affirmative action standards, "because of affirmative action demands, certification tests have been made more 'job relevant.' "[9] All applicants for positions at affirmative action employers benefit from this change.

If a business has set up qualification standards based solely on the performance and lifestyles of white males, it should not come as a surprise that other white males will be deemed most qualified in future applications. By examining those assumptions and making room for more flexible work standards, businesses open themselves to new skills and creative ways of solving problems not present in a monocultural work environment.

Regardless of issues raised by biased qualification standards, it is simply not true that people of color applying for jobs are statistically less well-qualified than members of the dominant culture. For example, during the 1970s and early 1980s, African-Americans in professional and managerial positions had an average of 14.8 years of education while their white counterparts averaged only 13.2.[10]

Affirmative action pushes employers to examine their qualification practices and assumptions. When vigorously pursued, this process of examination can open the door to a stronger, more flexible workforce.

Question #5: What about quotas?

In recent years politicians have lambasted hiring quotas. Quotas have been presented as unfair, restrictive, demeaning means to a doubtful end.

I will not dive into full-scale discussion of quotas. But I will make two observations and ask a few questions.

My first observation is that quotas and affirmative action are frequently used synonymously. This is misleading. Affirmative action programs span a broad range of options including—but not limited to—starting good faith efforts, validating qualification requirements, implementing recruitment strategies, and establishing numerical goals. Rarely does a program mandate that "x" number of people of color must be hired in "y" number of months. Instead, the numerical goals, quotas if you must, set a mark to measure progress by.

Second, without those goals, companies can simply point to all their good intentions and say they have implemented an affirmative action program. As with dismantling racism, our words and intentions are only as good as the results. We must certainly allow time for changes to come about, but as the early years of affirmative action showed, progress can be achieved in far less time than some of us might otherwise allow ourselves.

Now the questions. Why are people so upset about racial quotas at educational institutions and businesses but not about other forms of preference? Many schools, including Harvard and Yale, set aside a given number of "legacy" placements for each entering freshman class. These sons and daughters of wealthy alumni are never labeled "unqualified," even though their academic credentials may be open to question, since there is less competition for these privileged slots.

And what about the "good ole' boy" network? As Kathleen Parker of the National Center for Career Strategies points out, 86 percent of all available jobs do not appear in the classified advertisements.[11] Clearly many people get jobs because they have met the quota of knowing the right person at the right time. Criticism of numerical goals set up to bring about diversity in the workplace becomes feeble in light of many other "quotas" filled through personal and family contact.

Question #6: Whose coffee is it?

I began this chapter with the story of the coffee dispenser in the convenience store. In the story, I identify most with Joe. Like him, I move directly and purposefully toward my goals. Sometimes I assume that I have a right to a goal simply because I have set my hopes on achieving it. Like Joe moving toward the coffee machine, I assume that if no one is following the same path I am, they don't deserve to achieve the goal before me.

For example, I may apply for a job in a company that already has many people like myself on staff, people who have taken the same path I did to obtain their current positions. My qualifications are in order. I go in to an interview believing I am the best person for the job. I may assume that the coffee, the goal, the job are mine. I deserve them. Then I learn I will have to wait in line for another job opportunity.

The one that was "mine" has gone to someone who took another path to get to the same place. From the perspective of my aisle in the convenience store, it looked like no one else was in the aisle with me. I forgot to pay attention to the whole store. As it turned out, others had taken a different route and were moving toward the same place. Their life experience and training, while different than mine, made them equally strong candidates for the position. Despite our similar qualifications, the other person is given the job because she brings new perspectives and skills to the company. My skills and cultural insight were already widely represented among the company's present employees.

Members of the dominant culture have long assumed that all the jobs and all the coffee were theirs for the taking. They just had to wait their turn in the aisle. When doors that have long remained shut are opened to other aisles, it will initially seem that the "others" are butting in line, invading "our" turf, taking away "our" coffee. That transition will be difficult for all.

Eventually, I believe, the aisles will be broadened to include more room for those who have been shut out. We will of course need to pay attention to issues of power and privilege all along. Yet by examining the first assumption, "Whose coffee is it?" we will move a little closer to the river.

Question #7: How do we all benefit?

We have seen one way everyone benefits from affirmative action programs—certification tests have been made more "job relevant." Likewise, training programs put in place by many large corporations to meet affirmative action standards have benefited not only people of color but everyone working at those corporations. Statistics indicate that white women have benefited from affirmative action programs more than any other group.

Individual businesses, educational institutions, and society as a whole benefit from affirmative action programs as well. Businesses gain the resources to relate to wider cultural circles.

Likewise, by recruiting new workers from previously un-thought-of labor sources, such as colleges with large racial ethnic enrollment, businesses gain a whole new pool of qualified workers. Educational institutions benefit from increased cultural diversity and the ensuing cross-cultural interaction that stimulates. Society becomes more vibrant as the gifts and skills of people of color are valued and included in public discourse and function.

Additionally, if affirmative action programs live up to their full potential, many of the unexamined assumptions that undergird white privilege in the context of racism will be challenged. In addition to examining assumptions of qualification, increased workplace interaction forces people to work together and provides opportunity for building friendships across cultural lines.

We must be careful, however, not to expect too much of affirmative action programs. There are plenty of dangers. Paternalism, closed communication channels, and lack of opportunity for advancement are just a few of the problems that can develop. Affirmative action is an important tool but not the only one. It can never be substituted for work at dismantling the systems of racism and white privilege so deeply ingrained into society.

Question #8: Must there always be winners and losers?

I have noted one fallacy of viewing affirmative action as a race to the coffee pot—the assumption that there is only one way, one aisle, to get to the coffee pot. Another fallacy is that it sets up a competition in which one must lose and one win. This need not always be the case.

If we say that only one job is available and must be done from eight to five, five days a week, we will find it hard to break out of a win-lose equation. But breaking out of traditional work strictures allows options previously not considered to emerge.

One business faced with an economic forecast that required employee layoffs decided not to proceed in the usual fashion of last hired, first fired (or laid off). Having recognized that those most recently hired included a greater number of people of color because of relatively recent implementation of affirmative action, the company lay off people on a more proportionate basis by racial groupings.

Another business distributed the layoff burden through a program of work sharing. Instead of laying off one person out of every five people, every five workers worked four days and collected unemployment the fifth day.[12]

Similar options that break out of the five-day-a-week work mold can be used to create employment opportunities, not just make layoffs more equitable. With creativity and a continuing openness to examining issues of power and privilege, we can escape the win-lose model.

Question #9: We already have affirmative action. What more do we need?

Once an active affirmative action program has been instituted and goals are being met, the job is far from done. Other areas to be examined include office location, working hours, paid holidays, dress codes, work cycles, communication patterns, supply vendors, and market arenas.[13]

For example, if an office is located in a suburb far from mass transit systems, applicants with no access to individualized transportation will automatically be excluded. Similarly, business consultant Bahati Ansari encourages to make the work environment more comfortable for people from outside the dominant culture. She "encourages workplaces to recognize other religions' holidays; permit different cultural dress . . . and offer flextime schedules."[14] The latter in particular allows parents with small children to share child care responsibilities.

Neither does everyone go about work in the same way. Some cultures place a higher value on relationship building than on task completion. While one worker may plow into a project Monday morning, another may take time at the beginning of the day to catch up on how co-workers spent their weekends. In most cases, both will finish their work, but one eases up at the end of the day rather than taking extra time at the beginning.

This is not to imply that people of one culture or another always fit a particular pattern. As we have examined earlier, there is abundant variety within each culture. At the same time, when many cultures come together, the variety increases and it becomes even more essential to examine the assumptions behind work cycles and communication patterns.

There are three more areas to examine in the workplace—supply vendors, market arenas, and advertising images. Who supplies the raw materials for a manufacturing plant, the paper and pens for an office, or the produce for a grocery? Why have they been chosen? Are there other vendors owned by members of racial ethnic communities that could use the consistent support of a stable company?

In the same way, what assumptions have been made about marketing the product, searching out clientele, or stocking the shelves? For example, are bilingual automatic tellers available in Hispanic communities? Likewise, is it really true that racial ethnic community members are poor risks for lending institutions? (Financial evidence indicates otherwise.)

All of these examples demonstrate how much work remains for all businesses and institutions as we seek to end racism and respond to an increasingly diverse work force. More and more models of change become available as time goes on. We can no longer use the excuse that we want to do better but don't know how. In addition to many positive examples, several of them referred to above, countless resources are available to continue moving toward the healing river.

Question #10: But what about Seth?

We have all heard a story like the one Seth Thomas (not real name) told me.

After teaching geophysics in a midwestern university for a number of years, Seth found out about a college teaching opening. Representatives of the school told him to apply for the position. "You're our first choice," they told him.

A few months later, he received a very different message. "We're sorry, but we have to hire a minority," he was told. "However, if two others turn it down, we'll give it to you." Then that message changed as well. "If we do give it to you, it will just be a temporary position until we get a minority person in there."

The position went to a well-qualified person, but he was not from a traditional North American racial ethnic group. An upper-class professor from Asia received the job. "I wouldn't have minded as much if the job had not been given to someone who came from a privileged background. It would be like I went to England and was given a teaching position just because I was from another country," Seth ruminated.

This is a painful story for Seth to share. He has not found a teaching position. Yet Seth feels God has called him to teach and it is what he has always wanted to do.

How do we make sense out of this story given what we know about white privilege, racism, and affirmative action? Is it possible to view this account as anything but a frustrating example of affirmative action gone awry?

One other piece of information needs to be told. The school was under court order to desegregate. Another state university, a sister school, was primarily African-American, whereas the school Seth applied to was primarily European-American. There was pressure for new positions to go to people of color.

Was it wrong that Seth was not given the job, especially when told he would probably get the position? Seth believes telling him he was first choice was a mistake. And he could have understood if an African-American or Hispanic had received the position. An entire history of segregation needed to be systemically addressed. Yet in this instance, while the institution may have met its goal of hiring more people of color, the question remains whether the hiring of a privileged member of another country really met the original purpose of affirmative action.

There will be more stories like this as affirmative action measures are applied and racism is undone. Job opportunities will probably be less readily available for white males. There will be instances of seeming disparity if not outright unfairness.

Are these issues of oppression? I do not think so. Will they be painful and difficult for those unable to find jobs in areas they hope to work? Yes. Is this "reverse racism"? No. As long as white privilege remains, as long as white people hold the power of economics, politics, and influence, such instances cannot be put in the same category as the racism that has oppressed people of color for centuries. Such racism that has murdered millions, re-stricted millions, and denied opportunity to millions more.

The church must give its best energy to ending racism. This will mean providing resources and support for racial ethnic communities in their struggle for self-determination. But where creative options to avoid the win/lose dichotomy are not possi-ble, the church must also stand with those dominant culture members who have been displaced.

I pray for the day when an African-American woman can be hired for a leadership position and no one will even hint at the possibility she received it because of affirmative action. I also pray for the day when workplaces will be diverse enough and power distributed equitably enough that a European-American male can be hired for a leadership position and no one will even hint at the possibility he received it because of racism.

The first will have to come before the second. But they both will come. The healing river cannot be stopped.

11

So What Can We Do About Racism?

DYLAN MOSES is our first-born. At the time of this writing, the memory of his second birthday is just two months old. Dylan likes to hold his brother Zachary, has recently taken an interest in singing while holding the *Mennonite Hymnal* in his lap, and relishes a bowl of cold cereal and milk for breakfast.

Dylan is as white a little boy as they come. With light-toned skin, blond hair, and blue eyes, he matches the pictures of "typical" little boys in many an elementary school primer of old. He has what used to be called "the all-American look."

Fortunately for all of us, many elementary texts now picture children from a variety of ethnic backgrounds. In contrast to when I was in first grade, Dylan will probably see children from a broad variety of cultures represented in his textbooks. He and Marjorie Ann, daughter of a friend of ours, will likely see pictures of children with skin the color of peaches like Dylan's, the color of plums like Marjorie Ann's, and all the colors in between.

Likewise, the assumptions that gave preference to people with the blond-haired, blue-eyed "all-American look" have begun to be challenged. People are recognizing that the "all-American look" also refers to skin hues of the fullest brown, warmest yellow, and richest black. Each one can be valued without diminishing the beauty of the others.

Dylan doesn't yet know he is white. He doesn't differentiate between people based on racial characteristics. During the nine months he spent in day care, starting at age one, he was completely unaware he was the only white child there. When Dylan does become aware of differences in skin color, physical ability, accent, and gender of the people around him, we hope to encourage him to acknowledge those differences and value them. We want him to develop an understanding of the inherent unfairness of bias. As he grows older, we also want him to understand how his people have been afflicted with racism in hopes he might be freed of the disease.

We probably won't have that difficult of a time encouraging Dylan to appreciate diversity. Children have a natural openness to the world around them, a curiosity about differences. They are taught attitudes of bias. They are not born with them.

At a reception celebration we held in honor of Zachary's dedication, Dylan and Marjorie Ann sat together and looked at a pop-up book about the zoo. They have not developed the fears, hesitancies, and subtle prejudices so many of us adults carry into cross-cultural interaction. Dylan Moses and Marjorie Ann encourage Cheryl and me and Marjorie's mother, Juanita, to set our fears aside and do something about racism.

Because of my children

The more I learn about racism, the more I see it is deeply entrenched in our church, society, and world. Change will take hard work. Dylan and Marjorie Ann give me hope to engage in that work. Although the fruit of my work will not be fully harvested in my lifetime, I hope Dylan and his friends can enjoy its taste. As with the coming of the kingdom, we rejoice in the bits and pieces we see now, knowing we may not see the fullness of the kingdom in our lifetime. And we recognize that even our best efforts will mean nothing unless rooted in God's grace.

Even as God gives good grace, God has also given us many courageous examples of people working to dismantle racism. I had no trouble collecting stories and examples of people who have entered the healing river.

As you read this chapter, you will notice I have chosen stories from both dominant culture and racial ethnic communities. By telling both sorts of stories, I hope to show that all of us need to work together to move toward the healing river. Certainly the strategies and action we choose will take different forms in different places. But the tie that holds our action together needs to be our common understanding of white privilege, prejudice, and power. Without this understanding, we risk furthering the problems we seek to end.

If we work together, we become more than one or two individuals floundering in the water. Through common effort, we add to the ever-growing movement in the healing river. We must consciously join others involved in the same work we are. If we swim alone, we either tire and sink or climb out of the river to more comfortable ground.

I hope this chapter will serve as an invitation to join the movement in the healing river. The stories included here will allow you to meet some who have been swimming for a long time. They will tell you of the examples, strategies, and experiences that have kept them afloat.

Personal relationships

At the heart of dismantling racism is commitment to building relationships of equality across cultural and ethnic lines. The church can be a place where those relationships grow and flourish. Educational institutions, the workplace, and community groups also offer opportunities for entering into new cross-cultural relationships—but given housing patterns and social circles, those relationships rarely drop into our laps. We must create opportunities for developing relationships by seeking out places where different ethnic groups come together, then moving outside of our safety zones to get to know new people.

The many church services, work projects, gospel sings, and community events we attended in New Orleans gave us a wealth of friends and contacts that extend far beyond our Swiss-

Germanic roots. As an introvert, it takes energy for me to enter a new environment. As a parent of small children, it takes even more energy to ready our family to attend a gospel sing on a Sunday afternoon when a nap and a long walk seem far more inviting. However, I usually leave such cross-cultural experience far more energized than when I arrived.

Church services, parties, and personal relationships involving people from many cultures stir me to consider again the wonder and joy awaiting us as the healing river flows over this land. A wedding of two former MCC service workers in New Orleans brought together a wonderful blend of culture and ethnicity. Old friends and new acquaintances gathered in a Methodist gymnasium on the outskirts of the French Quarter to sample foods as different as Creole jambalaya and German whoopie pies, to listen to music as wide-ranging as Cajun zydeco and Jewish klezmer, to recognize faiths as distinct as Mennonite and Roman Catholic, and to learn to know people from communities as diverse as Lancaster County and New Orleans Ninth Ward. In the midst of all of this, I couldn't help but give glory to God for the wonderful gifts of culture.

As I remember that celebration and the many friendships across cultural lines that I've been privileged to develop, I'm reminded of a suggestion Tom Skinner makes. He says,

> It's in hanging out that I start unveiling the deep things in my life that I don't normally talk about. It's in hanging out that people get to know me and I get to know them. And it's in hanging out that I know where the other person is coming from. I learn their history and what they think.[1]

Perhaps what we need in our churches and workplaces is simply more time to be together free of structured agenda and other work. Relationships can be built in the midst of work, but authentic friendships also benefit from informal socializing.

An ecumenical group of churches in Milwaukee illustrates the benefits of such socializing. The Interfaith Conference of Greater Milwaukee has sponsored an extended series of workshops and evening sessions on racism coupled with a system of "ally-pairs." These ally-pairs are included as a means for people to break out of same race relationships.

Blacks and whites participating in the workshops are paired, then asked to spend a specific number of hours together in social settings of common interest. Initially the participants are placed in a larger cluster with two or three other pairs for common group activity. They are then encouraged to split off in ally-pairs for further interaction. Participants report many opportunities to get to know people they would not otherwise have met.

Allies along the way

The planners of the Milwaukee workshops purposefully chose the word "ally" to describe the pairs they set up. Roberto Chene, director of the Southwest Center for Cross-Cultural Relationships, has described some of the characteristics of an ally in the context of cross-cultural relationships. His list provides direction and insight for European-Americans who have become aware of white privilege and are looking for ways to dismantle racism.

An ally—
1. Understands the nature of structural oppression.
2. Chooses to align with the victims of oppression.
3. Believes that it is in his/her self-interest to be an ally.
4. Is committed to the practice of the personal growth which is required.
5. Is quick to take pride and appreciate any successes.
6. Realize those we ally with are capable of taking care of themselves.
7. Is able to acknowledge and articulate how their patterns operate in practice, without self-blame.
8. Expects to make mistakes but does not use it as an excuse for nonaction.
9. Knows that each side in an ally relationship has a clear responsibility for their own change whether or not the other person changes.
10. Knows that in the most empowered ally relationship

that person(s) in the traditionally dominant role initiates the change toward personal and institutional equality.

11. Knows that he/she is responsible for humanizing or empowering their role in the institution, particularly as that role relates to minorities.

12. Promotes a sense of community where she or he works.

13. Has a good sense of humor.[2]

I particularly like the last line. If we can't do the work with the ability to laugh at ourselves, it will be a long journey. Racism has sorely afflicted this land, but the healing river cannot do its work if we are always dour and depressed.

I remember how laughter helped me heal. When I was in Costa Rica as a college junior, my appendix quit. In the midst of considerable pain, I was admitted to a San José hospital. The morning after the appendectomy I lay in bed feeling lonely and depressed. Unexpectedly, a group of my classmates came to visit. They told jokes for the next half-hour. It hurt to laugh, but I sure felt better afterward. May we all discover the gift of laughter as we work to find healing from the disease of racism.

What does an ally look like?

Becoming an ally takes many forms. According to vocation, family responsibility, and personality, ally action will vary greatly. Even so, it is possible to learn from those who have acted to bring about healing from racism. Here is the story of one person working to become an ally.

In the spring of 1992, Neil Avenue Mennonite Church (Columbus, Ohio) sponsored a seminar on racism entitled "All God's Children Are Precious." The weekend event featured worship, plenary sessions on cross-cultural relations and white privilege, children's activities, and workshops on topics as far-ranging as "Interracial Adoption," "Black and Mennonite," and "African-American Worship." Sixty people from throughout Ohio attended the seminar and gave positive reviews.

Robin Walton, one of the event's principal organizers, told

the story of her experience preparing for the seminar and working as an ally.

> I felt very self-conscious making calls last fall about developing a conference on racism. As a representative of a practically all-white congregation, I was convinced that the response I would get would be, "Why now? Where were you when we needed you before?"
>
> But reactions were much different, even from pastors who have been about this work for a very long time. To them the timing seemed perfect. And they seemed relieved that someone else was taking the lead.
>
> As I began looking for resource people, I discovered that each of the people I spoke with had a nugget of truth clarified through their work in undoing racism. Something bigger than our puny conference had begun to take shape. We were pulling together a network of people, of ideas, of God's wisdom. We were about God's work.
>
> In our planning, we linked with the Lee Heights Community Church in Cleveland, Ohio, a predominantly African-American church with Mennonite connections. Out of this spirit of cooperation and trust, we gathered about sixty people from around the state, learned from each other, and grew together.

Robin and several others involved in planning the conference have taken part in a racial unity task force in Columbus. The task force is made up of members from churches throughout the city. They share four services a year focusing on racial reconciliation. The services follow the normal worship and singing style of the hosting congregation, but a guest minister preaches the sermon. For example, a black Baptist service might feature a white Methodist preacher and vice versa.

After one service held soon after the 1992 Los Angeles rebellions, a group of about forty people came together to listen to each other. "The group ranged from a white woman asking, 'Just what is the problem here?' to an African-American youth sharing his story of not being able to achieve his goals because of racism," Robin recalled. She is part of a subcommittee looking at ways to keep the dialogue going.

Corporate action

Another way allies can be intentional about commitment to change is through deliberate corporate action in response to situations of injustice. The story that follows, contributed by Melanie Zuercher, gives an example of a group of people responding in this way.

Sometime in late 1987 or early 1988, when Jesse Jackson was running for president, he made a campaign stop in Hazard, Kentucky, county seat of Perry County. As in many eastern Kentucky counties, the percentage of African-Americans in Perry is small. Nearby Harlan County, with an African-American population of ten to fifteen percent, probably has the highest representation in the region.

Nevertheless, it had been over a decade since a political figure of national status had come to eastern Kentucky, and Jackson's visit generated much excitement in Hazard. He gave a speech to a packed house and took advantage of a number of photo opportunities. One was at a Hazard landmark, Bailey's Restaurant and Tire Store. The restaurant was famous for its homemade pie, a piece of which Jackson was snapped sampling.

In the summer of 1990, the Southern Empowerment Project (SEP), a six-week training program for community organizers, held its Week 1 training in eastern Kentucky. (SEP is supported by several citizens groups in Kentucky, Tennessee, and North Carolina. The organization for which I work, Kentuckians for the commonwealth [KFTC], was hosting the Week 1 training.)

One day the organizer interns, a trainer, and an SEP staffer stopped for lunch at Bailey's. I met the group there, arriving at least ten minutes after they did. I sat down with the trainer and an intern, all of us white. Several other interns were sitting at a nearby table. Several of them were African-American and the rest were white.

My table was waited on almost as soon as I sat down. Our food arrived quickly. Only as we were eating did we notice that the table with the African-American interns did not have food yet. They had not even been waited on.

That table only received service after everyone else in the KFTC group and several customers who came in later had been served. When at last service came, it was in order of skin color— the person with the darkest skin got her food last.

The SEP staffer was in another room, unaware of what was happening. Only when the group returned to the training center did he learn about the incident.

At that point the training was suspended and the planned curriculum abandoned. The group went into a planning and action session to discuss and analyze the racist incident. They struggled with the issue into the next morning.

Deciding to confront the manager, they called to tell her they were coming and why. As the group walked across the parking lot into the restaurant, one of the manager's sons met them and made threatening remarks. They went on.

The group demanded an apology and reimbursement of the bill and tip. The manager cried and said she hadn't meant to hurt anyone's feelings. She and the waitress who had served the table apologized for the "misunderstanding." Both insisted they had not been racist. They offered to reimburse the tip but the group said all or nothing and left without the money.

Although the results of the action weren't completely satisfactory, the group felt the confrontation had been important and that by acting together they had overcome the powerlessness many of them had felt after the incident. Later several white KFTC leaders, who had not been at the restaurant but had been part of subsequent events, said this experience had been a turning point in their views of racism.

Action in Caesar's realm

As Melanie's story demonstrates, deliberate action in response to overt incidents of racism often leaves us empowered and energized. By taking such action, we refuse to allow feelings of powerlessness to hold sway. Action builds hope.

If we remain open to responding to racist actions around us, we are inevitably faced with the choice of how we will operate in Caesar's realm. How will our understanding of racism affect our involvement in the public arena? In particular, what does it tell us about our response to three key areas—media images and reporting, corporate policies that impact communities of color, and decisions made by our governmental leaders?

In each area, white people need to listen closely to the response coming from people of color involved with struggles for self-determination. As I move into more diverse cultural circles and develop authentic cross-cultural relationships, I begin to see public issues in a new light. What would previously have gone unnoticed becomes important to me. The more I understand that my healing as a white person is linked to the healing of people of color around me, the more I am concerned about decisions made, policies implemented, and media images projected.

Environmental racism is one issue affected by decisions made in each of these areas. While the mainline media have increasingly addressed environmental issues, they rarely provide information on the disproportionate impact of environmental hazards on people of color. The media have largely ignored the realities represented by the following statistics:

- in the U.S., 60 percent of the total African-American population and 60 percent of the total Hispanic population live in communities with one or more uncontrolled toxic waste sites;
- about half of all Asian/Pacific Islanders and Native Americans live in communities with uncontrolled toxic waste sites;
- lead poisoning endangers the health of nearly eight million inner-city children, the majority of them African-American and Hispanic.[3]

One reason news of this sort is not covered stems from corporate influence. For example, one network television executive refused to include footage about a contaminated well located in a Hispanic community in a program on environmental issues. When pressed, he explained that the corporation responsible for the well contamination had ties to his network.[4]

Likewise, the U.S. government's Environmental Protection Agency (EPA) has a lengthy history of negligence and inaction regarding concerns expressed by people of color. In July 1991, members of the Southwest Network for Environmental and Economic Justice confronted the EPA with well-documented evidence of this history of neglect. Instead of implementing non-discriminatory policies in regulation and enforcement as suggested, the head of the EPA initiated a media campaign to counter this image. Fortunately this duplicitous maneuver was exposed by a member of congress at the first press conference set up as part of the EPA's media campaign.[5]

Individual action can make a difference as well. But as we are tied into regional and national efforts to work against issues like environmental racism, our actions are amplified many times over. For those of us who look to the church for our base of involvement with the world, interdenominational efforts to undo racism hold hope for positive change.

I believe it is essential for the church to become involved in working to bring healing to such areas of woundedness in our world. As we within the Christian community become more diverse and interconnected across ethnic lines, we will seek healing without hesitation for all our sisters and brothers.

A brief stop at the office

We have spent an entire chapter examining one of the major workplace issues, affirmative action, but it may be helpful to make brief mention of follow-up questions we need to ask as our workforce becomes more diverse.

Where is your office located?
Who do you serve?
Who makes the decisions?
Where do you obtain your services?
Who do you work with?

Although immediately applicable to traditional business settings, these questions also can be applied to a hospital, heavy industry center, bookstore, churches, and most work settings.

As we struggle with how to answer these questions when racism and white privilege are the norm, the words of Horace Seldon, a long-time organizer for racial reconciliation, may be helpful.

> If those of us who are white continue to believe, perceive, analyze, and act the way we always have, then the result will be racism in the institutions we control or influence. To change those patterns requires intentional plans, implemented consistently over a long period of time.[6]

Reba's reconciling response

One church implementing a plan for racial reconciliation is in Evanston, Illinois. Over twenty years ago, Reba Place began as an intentional community. In the words of at least one early member, they were an "idealistic group who wanted to model our lives after the community of Acts." They shared an understanding of the world as focused on individualism, materialism, violence, and warfare, a world they wanted to witness to from a community base.

Evanston is similar to most North American suburbs. Almost all the churches are segregated. In the immediate neighborhood surrounding Reba Place, the population is evenly mixed between African-Americans and European-Americans. Through the years, members of Reba Place have tried many ways to bring their neighbors into their fellowship. In early 1991, several members felt a longing for more. They still felt they had not done everything they could to work at racial reconciliation.

Anne Stewart has been with Reba Place for twenty years. As an African-American, Stewart was aware that working at racial reconciliation would require significant resources. In the summer of 1991, Stewart helped lead an adult Sunday school class on racial reconciliation. "We shared profoundly in that group," Stewart recalled. "A number of people had worked at racial reconciliation in the past and carried considerable pain. They felt there wasn't a hopeful way."

This mixed group made up of thirty European-Americans and ten African-Americans provided the impetus needed to move Reba Place toward more significant work at racial reconciliation. Stewart added, "We were keeping with our mission of dealing with the sin of racism in our culture."

Living Hope Cluster, a gathering of four small groups, decided to accept the responsibility of conceiving a specific plan. They were an ordinary group of Christians. But they listened closely to the Spirit's leading and moved toward the extraordinary.

As they prayed and talked about what to do next, they decided they needed African-American male leadership. "We began a whole series of conversations with black male leaders and they confirmed what we had already set out to do. If we wanted to be serious, we needed black leadership," Stewart noted.

James Offutt accepted an invitation to provide leadership. Offutt works with a task group to welcome persons of color and meet the needs they have. "The group I work with is built right into the small group structure of the church," Offutt explained, "and this gives our work a validity it wouldn't have otherwise."

Julius Belser, one of Reba Place's pastors, remarked that Offutt's work "provides reconciling leadership across the city during a particularly tense time." He added, "There's no question this is going well. Energy and excitement are being maintained. Already the number of black people has quadrupled."

Of course they have not yet become a completely reconciled community. But they have listened to the direction of the Spirit as they begin the journey toward racial reconciliation. "We have to look at our worship form and church structure. It's real tricky when you have a majority/minority situation. We need to find ways to give up power to people of color," Stewart concluded. The fruit of the Spirit is not always easy to harvest, but the rewards far outweigh the cost.

One thing that gives me hope about the work members of Reba Place have done is that it has grown so naturally out of their life together. No one placed a guilt trip on them. Members of the church were moved to work because of their life experience and a longing for a more reconciled church. Likewise, no charismatic, famous speaker pushed them. They simply allowed God's Spirit to turn their ordinary lives into extraordinary ones.

Not every church's work at racial reconciliation will look the same. I expect, however, that many of these same elements of longing, ordinary people, and the fruit of the Spirit will be present in all such authentic response.

In the Foster home

Along with the public arena, workplace, and church, the family setting is another area in which we can do something about racism.

The first story I'd like to share shows again how relationships can affect our world view far more significantly than almost any other educational format.

Sandra and Brent Foster are therapeutic foster parents in their home in Elkhart, Indiana. They take in children who need a stable, loving home environment. Over several months, they see remarkable transformation in the children.

The process is not without pain, however. Foster described the dilemma he has observed in several of the children, "They don't know how to respond to love from people they have been taught to call 'niggers.' They have been taught to be racist to such an extent that they don't see we are taking them in when their own families can't care for them."

As the children learn they are accepted in the Foster home, they begin to understand that the stereotypes they have been taught are untrue. "Our kids had to grow, too," Foster commented, "because they carried stereotypes about 'white folks.' I encouraged my children to judge their foster brothers on the basis of their character, not on the color of their skin."

One time a foster son, Brandon, returned home from spending a weekend with his family of origin and told Sandra and Brent, "My grandaddy says he don't like niggers."

They responded, "Well, that means he doesn't like us."

Brandon's reaction was intense and immediate, "No, not you, not you."

"He had grown to know us as people, but was not yet able to see beyond race," Foster recalled.

Another time Brandon and the Fosters' oldest son, Michael, were watching television when a commercial came on about women's makeup. Brandon said that the black woman in the commercial was ugly and the white woman pretty.

"Michael got mad," said Foster, "so I told both of them they each would find members of their own culture more attractive, but that didn't make one woman more beautiful than the other. I told them some of us are lucky enough to see beauty everywhere in people from all ethnic groups."

After Brandon apologized, Foster asked him why he thought the black woman was ugly. He had no idea.

Despite difficult episodes, Sandra and Brent are rewarded by the changes they see in the children. Brandon occasionally stops by to say hello and express a longing to return. "He now knows that blacks are as full of love and caring as anyone else," Foster concluded, "so he has done what we all need to do. He has learned to see beyond race, to get to know people by more than skin color, to take risks that take him beyond his prejudices."

Raising up children in the way they should go

Two child educators, Louise Derman-Sparks and Herbert Kohl, have written at length about the many ways parents and educators of young children can encourage antibias development in their offspring and charges. Here are a few suggestions from Derman-Sparks:

- show that you value diversity in the friends you choose and in the people and firms you choose for various services;
- make it a firm rule that a person's identity is never an acceptable reason for teasing or rejection;
- talk positively about each child's physical characteristics and cultural heritage;
- respectfully listen to and answer children's questions about themselves and others;

- teach children to recognize stereotypes and caricatures of different groups;
- use accurate and fair images in contrast to stereotypic ones, and encourage children to talk about the differences;
- let children know that unjust things can be changed;
- involve children in taking action on issues relevant to their lives. Talk to a toy store manager or owner about adding more toys that reflect diversity, such as dolls, books, and puzzles. Ask your local stationary store to sell greeting cards that show children of color. Take your child to a rally about getting more funding for child care centers. As you involve children in this type of activity, be sure to discuss the issues with them, and talk about the reasons for taking action.[7]

In a related area, Kohl suggests that parents and educators pay careful attention to how stories from racial ethnic communities are presented. The story of Rosa Parks provides an example of how stories can be turned from their original purpose. As most of us are aware, Rosa Parks' refusal to sit in the back of a public bus sparked the struggle in Montgomery and throughout the South to desegregate public transportation. Kohl notes that the story is often misconstrued to reflect the individual act of a lone, tired seamstress cut off from a larger organized struggle for justice. He comments,

> To call Rosa Parks a poor tired seamstress and not talk about her role as a community leader as well, is to turn an organized struggle for freedom into a personal act of frustration. . . .
> They [the African-American leaders in Montgomery] were looking for someone who had the respect of the community and the strength to deal with the racist police force as well as all of the publicity that would result from being at the center of a court challenge to discrimination on buses.
> The story of collective decision making, willed risk, and coordinated action is more dramatic than the story of an

angry individual who sparked a demonstration. . . .
    Not every child can be a Rosa Parks, but everyone can
imagine her or himself as a participant in the boycott.[8]

I was much more impressed with the story of Rosa Parks
when I learned that she played a specific role in a large movement of oppressed peoples. She was chosen after careful delib-
eration and consideration. It was even more exciting to discover
that she had been involved in previous actions of resistance to
segregation in the South and had even received training at the
Highlander Retreat Center, a resource center for many leaders
of the civil rights struggle.
    Our children will gain far more from an accurate depiction of
such leaders than through any idealized version that tells the
story of an individual cut off from an organized movement for
change.

Of cost and commitment

In this chapter I have included several examples of committed allies, people, and groups who have entered the river and
sought healing from racism. Many other examples could have
been included. Each day more and more people are entering the
river. The actions they engage in take different forms in different
environments. Some learn to interrupt racist jokes told by co-
workers. Some advocate for a less Eurocentric form of education. Still others develop a sister church relationship with a congregation from a different ethnic background or organize
churches to oppose passage of particularly discriminatory legislation.
    The possibilities are numerous. As we enter action out of a
sense of hope and a desire for our own healing and the healing
of all, we will be able to sustain action over the many years it will
take to find healing from racism. The examples abound! We
have not even addressed how we can encourage more diversity
and complete coverage in the media, challenge monocultural
images in ecclesiastical imagery, or counter racism in the criminal justice system. The resource section at the end of the book

contains many examples of materials and groups available for furthering education and action.

Throughout this book I have tried to make clear my belief that the problem of racism is the problem of all people. We have all been touched by the disease and will only find healing by working together. Our actions will vary according to our ethnicity and experience, but they need to be tied together by a common understanding of white privilege, prejudice, and power. That common understanding will allow us to work together as a body of believers moving toward the healing river.

To the European-Americans who have read to this point, I reiterate my belief that we have much to offer and much to gain by seeking healing from racism. An exciting, invigorating journey to the river awaits us. There is also cost involved. Sometimes that cost will bring unexpected pain and uncertainty into our lives, but like the pain of laughter after an appendectomy, it brings healing.

The authors of *Creating a New Community: God's People Overcoming Racism* have written one of the clearest descriptions I have seen of what this cost entails.

> Doing something about racism in our lives, as persons and as communities, requires that we move beyond understanding the problem and even having compassion for its victims. Those who are excluded and dominated seek not pity but justice. They want nothing done for them but rather the transfer of power to do for themselves. The transfer of power means real change in the lives of those who benefit by the present arrangements of power. To care enough to share the pain of others, to make their exclusion and domination our own, to stand with them in witness and action against the system dividing and conquering us—this is the cost of combating racism.[9]

As I wrote the closing of this chapter, some of that cost touched me in a direct and personal way. I received the second of two responses regarding positions I had applied for in MCC. I was given neither job. In both cases, people of color were hired.

I believe those asked to do the work will fill the expectations of their job descriptions with distinction and beyond. At the same time, I am aware that the education that has taken place in MCC on white privilege, prejudice, power, and the need for increasing workplace diversity prepared the ground for recruiting the applicants who were hired. I would probably have had a better chance at being hired for one of those positions if that education had not taken place. Even as I rejoice that an organization I care for is beginning the long journey toward the healing river, I also must grieve a little loss in my life.[10]

This loss is nowhere near the scale of loss exacted from people of color, but it is a loss nonetheless. I pray my disappointment will move me to continued action and commitment to bringing about healing from racism. Together we will find healing. The river will not stop. Join in.

Afterword

THROUGHOUT THIS BOOK I have used metaphors that most help me get a handle on the slippery topic of racism. Frequently, I have referred to the images of healing river and racism as disease. Stories from my life, churches, and the Scriptures have filled out these metaphors.

As I cast about for a closing image that sums up the main ideas of this book, I keep returning to something that happened last night. Let me tell you a story about parenting, about a mistake I made, about my son Dylan and me.

Last night I yelled at Dylan.

It is not something I usually do. It is never something I want to do. But last night I did it.

I had barely finished washing the dishes when Dylan came into the kitchen with a box over his head, dropped two building blocks on the kitchen floor, and went back into his bedroom. I told him several times to please pick up the blocks so I could sweep the floor. Dylan remained in the bedroom, unmoving.

Feeling pressure to finish sweeping so I could help get the boys ready for bed, I asked him again. He didn't respond. I lost my temper. I yelled at Dylan, forced him over to the blocks, and made him pick them up.

After sweeping the floor, I apologized to Dylan and tried to explain to him why I had been so frustrated. He listened with the passing intensity only a two-year-old can muster. Then he gave me a hug, complete with several small pats on the back. He had a good bath, we read a few stories, and after a few sips of milk he went to bed.

Once Zachary settled down, Cheryl and I talked about how I could have handled the situation better. In the course of our discussion, it became apparent that, unlike Cheryl, I often interpret Dylan's refusal to respond to a request as an affront to my control. While Cheryl is equally concerned that Dylan learn to pick up his toys and respond to our requests, she is more flexible in her evaluation of the situation. If danger is involved, quick response is necessary. If only two blocks are involved, a more flexible approach is possible. Cheryl suggested I could have moved the blocks to the side until Dylan picked them up later.

I have a lot to learn about parenting. It doesn't come as naturally as I thought it would. Certainly the desire to be a good parent is there. I love Dylan and Zachary very much. Yet I do not become a better parent just by loving them more. I also become a better parent by learning communication skills and discipline methods that allow me to respond more creatively and consistently to incidents involving blocks on the kitchen floor.

I tell this story because it reminds me so vividly of my struggles with racism. To begin with, no one becomes a better parent or finds healing from racism just by reading books or going to workshops. While structured input and education is essential, theory alone just won't cut it. A parent is not a parent if he or she does not have children. We cannot find healing from racism if we do not work to bring an end to racist systems.

Likewise, only as we try to be better parents do we discover our shortcomings as parents; only as we seek healing from racism do we discover the extent of the disease. As I give Dylan guidance and care, I make mistakes, learn from those mistakes, and keep on trying. As I seek healing from racism, I discover that racism has affected me much more than I had thought. I have already told of learning more about my desire for control in the course of parenting Dylan. The discoveries have been no less significant in the course of working to dismantle racism.

While debriefing with co-trainers after a recent undoing racism workshop, I was helped to see the inaccuracy of an assumption I made during the training. I had told the group that a certain key analytical piece had been developed by a European-American, when, in fact, the insight had originated from a person of color many years before. I had assumed that the insight came from a white person, just as I often assume that certain inventions or discoveries in the scientific world have been made by white people. If I had not been actively involved with the struggle to undo racism, my assumption that only a white person could be so insightful would never have been challenged.

During such times of self-discovery, I also cast aside any sense of moral superiority over a parent who abuses a child or the European-American day laborer who pours gasoline over an African-American sales clerk and sets him on fire. While their actions are abhorrent, I recognize the seeds of abuse and violent racism within me. Fortunately I have been able to seek out healthy parenting models and resources on effective discipline so that I do not abuse my children. I've also been able to seek out healthy models of cross-cultural interaction and resources on dismantling racism so I do not engage in violent racism.

Furthermore, how we parent and how we dismantle racism are shaped by the systems around us. A parent forced to work two jobs to make ends meet will have less energy and patience to give to children. In communities that have just experienced a plant closing or other economic loss, people will look for scapegoats. Often people of color are those scapegoats. In addition to the economic system, our religious, political, and communication systems affect how we go about our work.

The comparisons go on. Past experiences affect both our parenting and our work at dismantling racism. Strong personal support systems allow us to work through the frustrations that come with parenting and dismantling racism. Observing other models gives us new ideas. Getting together with others involved with parenting or seeking healing from racism generates new techniques, strategies, and approaches. A solid grounding in a faith community can provide the vision and commitment needed to persevere.

One more comparison, perhaps the most important, needs to be told. In the end, I believe our struggle with racism (like our struggle with parenting, relationship, or becoming the church) is not so much a struggle of the moment as a struggle of the essence. And the essence—the heart of the problem, not just the outward aspect—is sin. We struggle with our individual sin, systemic sin, and the interplay of both. Yet in the midst of that struggle, grace pours down upon us. After I have yelled at Dylan, he hugs me. After discovering some of my prejudices, I take part in a multiethnic celebration of culture.

If you take nothing else from this book, know that in the midst of your struggle with racism grace will abound. As God reminded the apostle Paul, "My grace is sufficient for you, for power is made perfect in weakness" (2 Cor. 12:9a). This same God who healed Naaman, changed the water into wine, and raised Jesus from the dead will give us grace sufficient to our needs.

God created our differences. God also gave us the freedom to choose how to respond to them. Unfortunately, many have chosen to help create systems that give privilege to those with white skin. That need not stop us from choosing otherwise. We can enter into new friendships, encourage new church relationships, and challenge assumptions that hold those systems of white privilege in place.

God also created the healing river. I cannot get away from it. The river draws me on, moves me forward, washes over me, washes over us all.

Which river is this? The Mississippi and the Jordan. The power of love and the necessity of redemption. Our present, past, and future. The river flows through the heart of our nation and the soul of our belief. The river is the hope of racial reconciliation.

Appendixes

Appendix A: A Church of Many Peoples Confronts Racism

"Many Peoples Becoming God's People" is the theme of this joint gathering of the Mennonite Church and the General Conference Mennonite Church, August 1-6, 1989, in Normal, Ill. Our theme is an expression of our ethnic diversity and thus a cause for celebration. We are becoming more like the church for which our Lord prayed (John 17:11-12, 20-23; Eph. 11-22).

It is surely a gift of God's grace that the generations of Mennonites now living can witness the worship of our churches in North America in at least two dozen languages: Amharic, Arapaho, Blackfeet, Cantonese, Chinese, Cheyenne, Choctaw, Creole, Cree, English, French, Garifuna, High German, Hmong, Hopi, Indonesian, Laotian, Low German, Mandarin Chinese, Navajo, Saulteaux, Portuguese, Spanish, Taiwanese, Vietnamese, and others.

That some of these worship languages seem unfamiliar to many of us is merely a measure of our new beginnings toward a church of many peoples. We recognize with sorrow that we are part of a society established by invading the lands and the rights of earlier residents and by importing and enslaving other human beings. Many of our sisters and brothers, descendants of early victims, still suffer from the prejudicial attitudes of the majority and from economic and other manifestations of racial bias. At this gathering we are affirming in prayer, worship, and fellowship that we intend to become one church of many peoples. We recognize that our response to God's will in this matter will call for repentance from sinful attitudes in our own hearts. It will set us apart from some of the sinful directions of our North American societies, in Canada and the United States.

Racism is a particular social reality of evil our Lord asks us to confront in becoming God's people. There are those in our societies who actively promote racial strife and the domination of one race over others. Many resist equal opportunities for minorities in immigration, education, employment, and housing. Sometimes the social climate allows hate language in the public media, harassment on college campuses, gang beatings of minority people, defacing and arson of churches and synagogues, public demonstrations by hate groups, terrorism against minority means of livelihood, and even murder. The movements in many areas of North America to uphold English as the sole "official" language may tend to foster such hurtful racial attitudes and give sanction to unacceptable public behavior.

We reaffirm our previous statements, made in the 1960s, on various racial concerns (see Attachment 1). Yet too often we have been silent in the face of these injustices. We commit ourselves anew to witness and work for racial justice in our communities.

The foundation for our concerns is that we have become one in the blood of the crucified Christ (Eph. 2:14), and our membership is to be drawn from every race and tribe and language and nation (Rev. 5:9-10). Our public witness to this fact is an essential part of our evangelism. As representatives of Mennonite congregations throughout North America, we declare here and now that expressions and attitudes of racism are sin and are never acceptable in our Christian life. They must also not be accepted in silence in any of our personal, work, or leisure relationships.

As "Many Peoples Becoming God's People" churches, we

encourage our congregations to identify and speak out against all forms of racism in our communities. This will require study to recognize subtle forms of racism in the media, in social practices, housing and employment patterns, and even within the church. It will require us to learn to know and become known to the victims of racism who live among us so that we may publicly stand with them. Those who practice racial abuse and discrimination deprive themselves of the enriching variations God intended for the human family. We need to find ways to experience the joys and challenges of racial diversity through our social interactions and residential choices. Where congregations are predominantly of one race, initiatives should be taken to foster fellowship with congregations of other racial heritages. Where feasible, congregations should join in projects of common service and witness.

We confess that our church institutions—district and provincial conferences, churchwide and inter-Mennonite agencies, our colleges, camps, and health service centers—have not always escaped our society's pattern of institutional racism. We are called by the gospel to review our practices in employment, promotion, purchasing of materials, and inclusion of minorities on boards and committees. Where inequity is found, we need to repent, be reconciled, and take affirmative action to correct it.

At least once each year congregations can celebrate the richness of ethnic and racial diversity and examine anew ways we can combat the lingering racism in our society, in our church, and in ourselves. Opportunities for raising awareness may be found in the observance of World Fellowship Sunday on Pentecost (as promoted by the Mennonite World Conference) and celebration of a "Many Peoples Sunday." Other opportunities include the observance of Martin Luther King, Jr.'s, birthday[1] in the U.S. or remembrance of the Acadians[2] and Louis Riel[3] in Canada. Resources for congregational study was made available in 1989-1992 by the Commission on Home Ministries (GC) and the Board of Congregational Ministries (MC). CHM and BCM were asked to report on the usage of the resources to their respective 1991 and 1992 delegate assemblies.

We ask each congregation, district and provincial conference, board and commission of the Mennonite Church and General Conference Mennonite Church to give renewed attention to issues of racism. Particular encouragement and support is needed for the development of leadership of all ethnic and racial groups from local to churchwide levels.

The vision God gave Peter, that "God shows no partiality" (Acts 10:34), is still needed today. Let us pray for courage to be a people of God who fulfill that vision.

Attachment 1

1. "The Way of Christian Love in Race Relations," MC General Assembly, Aug. 24, 1955, Hesston, Kan.

2. "The Christian and Race Relations," GCMC Triennial Sessions, Aug. 12-20, 1959, Bluffton, Ohio.

3. "Reconciliation," MC General Assembly, Aug. 20-23, 1963, Kalona, Iowa.

4. "The Freedom Movement," GCMC Triennial Sessions, July 10-17, 1965, Estes Park, Colo.

5. "Urban Riots," MC General Assembly, Aug. 21-24, 1967, Lansdale, Pa.

6. "Urban-Racial Concerns," MC General Assembly, Aug. 18, 1969, Turner, Oreg.

Adopted by the Mennonite Church General Assembly and General Conference Mennonite Triennial Session, August 3, 1989. Used by permission.

Appendix B: Ten Ways to Make a Third-World Person Lose Effectiveness in an Organization

1. Staying One Up—Assuming that the person is in the job because he or she is a minority, not because he or she is qualified; making allowances for mistakes or low productivity because you did not expect much to begin with; viewing the cultural differences (talk, dress, styles, music, etc.) of third world-people as cultural deficiencies or as low class characteristics.

2. Generalizing—Viewing the mistakes of one third-world person as indicative of the whole race; assuming that one or a handful of blacks can speak or are speaking for all blacks; asking questions like, "What do you people think about such and such?" assuming that all blacks, Asians, Hispanics, or Indians look alike and think alike on all issues; expecting the third-world employee to take care of all minority concerns for the company.

3. Overprotecting—Applying lower standards because you don't expect them to perform as well as whites; discouraging them from taking risks trying to take on a difficult job; making decisions about transfers, promotions, etc., for them, because you wouldn't want them to fail or get hurt

4. Self-Protection—Not giving honest feedback, especially negative, to a third-world person; always needing to make the point that "I'm not prejudiced, my upbringing was different"; expecting credit for being "liberal."

5. Oversexualization—Assuming that all or most black women are unwed mothers or have a lot of children (the "Mammy Syndrome"), assuming that all Asian women are "Geisha girls"; assuming that all black men are desirous of white women, and arranging tasks and assignments so that white women and black men don't work together or travel together.

6. Forced Integration—Making an issue of the fact that third-world Employees eat lunch together, socialize together, etc.: perceiving that "they" are cliquish, or are segregating themselves, while simultaneously overlooking the fact that whites sit together and have their own social groups.

7. Ghettoizing—Hiring third-world people for support or

ancillary jobs that are out of the mainstream of the company, and that wield little power, i.e. EEO or Affirmative Action Office, Director of Community Relations, Director of Minority Affairs; assuming that minorities should only work with "their own kind," or work best with "their own kind."

8. Excluding, Ignoring, or Forgetting—Not dropping by to visit; not inviting them to lunch, not passing along information; not letting them know the inside "scoop" on how the organization really works; not giving them the supervision, coaching, training opportunities equivalent to that of white peers, not crediting their contributions, ideas, work in discussion with others, not shaking hands.

9. White Solidarity—Backing up a white person when they say or do something racist, and trying to minimize that behavior by telling the minority person that "he really is a nice guy, he's just a little prejudiced"; laughing along with racist jokes or remaining silent when a white person says or does something racist; not taking racist behavior seriously, and telling the minority victims of these incidents that he or she is overreacting or being too sensitive when they get upset.

10. Expecting to Be Taught—Using third-world people to teach me about my racism; expecting that if they want things to change, they should tell whites what they are doing wrong; asking them to keep me on my toes about language and action that may be racist; not taking responsibility for myself and learning about how I may be hurting others, on my own—rather than at their expense.

Excerpted from Rita Hardiman's, "Ten Ways to Make a Third-World Person Lose Effectiveness in an Organization," originally adapted from J. D. Palmer, "Ten Ways to Make a Woman Lose Effectiveness in an Organization."

Notes

Chapter One

1. *Peace Petitions: News for ELCA Peacemakers,* Winter 1991/92.

2. Joseph Barndt, *Dismantling Racism: The Continuing Challenge to White America* (Minneapolis, Minn.: Augsburg Fortress, 1991), 80.

3. Tim Wise, "Affirmative Action and the Politics of White Resentment," *Blueprint for Social Justice* 45 (October 1991): 4-5.

4. Ibid., 6.

5. Stanley W. Green, "How Do We Get Rid of Racism in the Mennonite Church?" *Gospel Herald* 85 (Feb. 11, 1992): 5.

6. "Foreign-born U.S. Population Rising," *The Times-Picayune,* May 30, 1992, A-17 (reprinted from *The Los Angeles Times*).

Chapter Two

1. Even as I make this choice, I recognize language is fluid. The terms I use may be out of date in a few years, if not months. There may be problems with the terminology I have chosen. I have, however, done my best to use those terms deemed fair and accurate as of this writing.

2. "Their Name Is Today," *Bread for the World in Louisiana* 10 (March 1992): 6.

Chapter Three

1. Many of the ideas in this section spring from a reading of Sam Keen's thoughts on enemy-making as represented in Tom Hampson and Loretta Whalen's, *Tales of the Heart: Affective Approaches to Global*

Education (New York: Friendship Press, 1991).

2. Yette, Samuel F. *The Choice: The Issue of Black Survival in America* (New York: Berkeley Publishing Corporation, 1971), 302.

3. Elizondo, Virgilio. *Galilean Journey: The Mexican-American Promise* (Maryknoll, N.Y.: Orbis Books, 1983), 51-52.

4. Ibid., 98.

Chapter Four

1. Brian Ogawa, *Color of Justice: Culturally Sensitive Treatment of Minority Crime Victims* (Sacramento, Calif.: Office of the Governor, State of California, 1990), 179-182.

2. I have decided not to try to list all the people involved in developing this definition of racism for fear of ignoring essential contributors. A heart-felt thanks goes out to all who have worked hard and risked much to help bring this analysis to more and more audiences.

3. "Dismantle Racism, Equipping Ourselves for a Lifetime of Struggle," *Synapses Messages* 11 (January/Feb. 1992): 1.

4. "Work Racism: The Color of Money," *The Times-Picayune*, Monday, Sept. 7, 1992.

5. "Stepping Up the War on Discrimination," *New York Times*, Nov. 1, 1987.

6. Gertrude Ezorsky, *Racism and Justice: The Case for Affirmative Action* (Ithaca, N.Y.: Cornell University Press, 1991), 25.

7. For further discussion of racial dynamics in the U.S. public education system, see Jonathan Kozol, *Savage Inequalities: Children in America's Schools* (New York: Crown Publishers, 1991).

Chapter Five

1. 1991 Census Bureau data (in thousands). U.S. households receiving food stamps, AFDC, or General Assistance: Total households—11,773. Total white households—7,253. Total black households—4,116. Total Hispanic—1,648. (Sum equal to more than total due to overlap between Hispanic and white households.)

2. 1991 Census Bureau data.

3. List of African-American contributions culled from Robert C. Hayden's *Eight Black American Inventors* (Reading, Mass.: Addison-Wesley, 1972); *Seven African-American Scientists* (Federick, Md.: Twenty-First Century Books, 1992); and *Eleven African-American Doctors* (Federick, Md.: Twenty-First Century Books, 1992).

4. See Jack Weatherford, *Indian Givers: How the Indians of the Americas Transformed the World* (New York: Ballantine Books, 1988).

5. Vincent Harding, *There Is a River: The Black Struggle for Freedom in America* (New York: Random House, 1981), 236.

6. Ibid., 234-235.

7. Robert B. Moore, *Racism in the English Language* (New York: The Racism and Sexism Resource Center for Educators, 1976), 11.

8. Moore, "Racist Stereotyping in the English Language," in *The Prison of Race and Gender*, 278.

9. See Dody S. Matthias, "Racism: From Guilt to Grace" (Minneapolis, Minn.: Augsburg Fortress, 1991).

10. Joseph Barndt, *Dismantling Racism: The Continuing Challenge to White America* (Minneapolis, Minn.: Augsburg Fortress, 1991), 152.

11. Cain Hope Felder, "Out of Africa I Have Called My Son," *The Other Side* 28 (November—December 1992): 10.

12. Rita Hardiman, "Ten Ways to Make a Third World Person Lose Effectiveness in an Organization," originally adapted from J. D. Palmer, "Ten Ways to Make a Woman Lose Effectiveness in an Organization" as included in "The Exchange Project," 1990 resource packet from the Peace Development Fund.

13. "Youth and the Military: A Guide for Activists" (Nyack, N.Y.: Fellowship of Reconciliation), 2-3.

14. Tony Brown, "Peacemaking from My Perspective," in *In Search of Peace: A Challenge from Four Non-White North American Mennonites*, ed. Emma LaRoque (Akron, Pa.: Mennonite Central Committee U.S. Peace Section, 1976), 7.

Chapter Six

1. Peggy McIntosh, *White Privilege and Male Privilege: A Personal Account of Coming to See Correspondences Through Work in Women's Studies* (Wellesley, Mass.: Peggy McIntosh, Center for Research on Women, Wellesley College, 1988), 4.

2. Stanley W. Green, "How Do We Get Rid of Racism in the Mennonite Church?" *Gospel Herald* 85 (Feb. 11, 1992): 5.

3. Brian Ogawa, *Color of Justice: Culturally Sensitive Treatment of Minority Crime Victims* (Sacramento, Calif.: Office of the Governor, State of California, 1990), 82.

4. Elliott Currie, *Confronting Crime: An American Challenge* (New York: Pantheon Books, 1985), 153.

5. *Black Enterprise* (August 1981), cited in *Fact Sheets on Institutional Racism* (New York: The Council on Interracial Books for Children, Inc., 1985), 14.

6. "Percent Distribution of Single—Offender Victimizations Based

on Race of Victims, by Type of Crime and Perceived Race of Offender," *Criminal Victimization in the United States, 1990* (U.S. Department of Justice, Office of Justice Programs, Bureau of Justice Statistics), 61.

7. See *Confronting Crime* or Howard Zehr, *Changing Lenses: A New Focus for Crime and Justice* (Scottdale, Pa.: Herald Press, 1990) for helpful discussions of crime and workable alternatives to the current criminal justice system.

8. Horace Seldon, *Racism: Negative Effects on Whites* (Boston: Community Change, Inc., 1992).

9. *National Council on Crime and Delinquency Focus* (June 1992), 7.

10. Ron Hiller and Judy Millar, "I Wish I Were . . . ," *Lunchbag Lizard* (Racine, Wisconsin: Western Publishing Company, 1990). Used by permission.

11. I am indebted to professor Peggy McIntosh for her critique of monocultural education in her paper "Interactive Phases of Curricular and Personal Re-Vision with Regard to Race" Working Paper, #219 (Wellesley, Mass.: Wellesley College Center for Research on Women, 1990).

Chapter Seven

1. I need to credit Robert Terry for stating so clearly, "To be White in America, is not to have to think about it," in "The Negative Impact on White Values," *Impacts of Racism on White Americans*, eds. Benjamin P. Bowser and Raymmond Hunt (Newbury Park, Calif.: Sage Publications, 1981), 120.

2. Those wishing to study the development of the use of white as a collective term should consult Winthrope D. Jordan, *White Over Black* and A. Leon Higginbotham, Jr., *In the Matter of Color: Race and the American Legal Process—The Colonial Period*. Billings and Washington have based much of their ongoing research on these texts.

3. Lois Bartel, *A New Vision: A Study in White Racism* (Scottdale, Pa.: Mennonite Publishing House; Newton, Kan.: Faith & Life Press, 1973), 16.

4. Andrew Hacker, "The Myths of Racial Division" *The New Republic* (Mar. 23, 1992): 25.

5. Ibid., 25.

6. Peggy McIntosh, "White Privilege: Unpacking the Invisible Knapsack," *Peace and Freedom* (July/August 1989): 10-12.

7. Orrin Ross, letter to the editor printed in *The Times-Picayune*, Wednesday, Oct. 2, 1991.

8. Thanks to professor Wilma Bailey for information on the Jordan.

9. Parts of this chapter as well as part of the introduction to the resource list at the end of this book first appeared in *Builder: An Educational Magazine for Congregational Leaders* (Jan. 1993) as "Racism and a Running White Boy," "The Paradox of the White Race," and "Talking about Racism: An Educator's Primer."

Chapter Eight

1. Liang Ho, *Cross-Cultural Swinging: A Handbook for Self-Awareness and Multi-Cultural Living* (Honolulu: Liang Ho, 1990), 4.

2. Roberto Chene, excerpted from mimeograph, "Multiculturalism: Implementation Perspective," (Albuquerque: Southwest Institute for Cross-Cultural Relationships, 6/25/91).

3. Dody S. Matthias, "Racism: From Guilt to Grace," ed. Shane Groth and Elise K. Nelson, *Adult Forum Series* (Minneapolis, Minn.: Augsburg Fortress, 1991), 6.

Chapter Nine

1. Richard K. MacMaster, *Land, Piety, Peoplehood* (Scottdale, Pa.: Herald Press, 1985), 42.

2. Ibid., 43.

3. Theron Schlabach, *Peace, Faith, Nation: Mennonites and Amish in Nineteenth Century America* (Scottdale, Pa.: Herald Press, 1988), 340.

4. Macmaster, 101.

5. Ibid., 101.

6. Schlabach, 35.

7. James Horsch, ed., *Mennonite Yearbook & Directory, 1992*, vol. 80 (Scottdale, Pa.: Herald Press, 1992), 210.

8. Lois Barrett, *The Vision and the Reality: The Story of Home Missions in the General Conference Mennonite Church* (Newton, Kan.: Faith & Life Press, 1983), 30.

9. Ibid., 30.

10. Rafael Falcón, *The Hispanic Mennonite Church in North America 1932-1982* (Scottdale, Pa.: Herald Press, 1986), 71.

11. Le Roy Bechler, *The Black Mennonite Church in North America 1886-1986* (Scottdale, Pa.: Herald Press, 1986), 73.

12. Ibid., 50.

13. Hershberger, Guy F. "Mennonites and the Current Race Issue," mimeograph copy of report (Sept. 10, 1963), 11-12.

14. Ibid., 22.

15. Brent E. Foster, Noel Santiago, Carlos Romero, *Developing Harmony Through Diversity* (Elkhart, Ind.: Mennonite Board of Congrega-

tional Ministries and Mennonite Board of Missions), 13.

16. Ibid., 13-14.

17. Hubert L. Brown, *Black and Mennonite: A Search for Identity* (Scottdale, Pa.: Herald Press, 1976), 73.

18. "Bringing Racism to Center Stage," *Gospel Herald* 84 (Nov. 5, 1991): 3.

19. Ibid., 3.

20. William Stringfellow, *An Ethic for Christians and Other Aliens in a Strange Land* (Waco, Tex.: Word Books, 1973), 138.

Chapter Ten

1. *Times-Picayune*, May 25, 1990.

2. I am heavily indebted to the work of Tim Wise and Gertrude Ezorsky for several of the points made in this chapter. Their contributions are woven throughout the chapter.

3. Horace Seldon, "A Context for Understanding the Current Attack on Affirmative Action," *Convictions About Racism in the United States of America: Essays and Articles by Horace Seldon* (Boston: Community Change, Inc., 1992), 46.

4. Theodore Cross, *The Black Power Imperative: Racial Inequality and the Politics of Nonviolence* (New York: Faulkner, 1984), 488.

5. Stephen L. Carter, *Reflections of an Affirmative Action Baby* (New York, N.Y.: Basic Books, 1991), 72.

6. Tim Wise, "Affirmative Action and the Politics of White Resentment," *Blueprint for Social Justice* 45 (November 1991): 1.

7. Ibid.

8. Eloise Hiebert Meneses, "The Roots of Racism," unpublished manuscript, 1.

9. Gertrude Ezorsky, *Racism and Justice: The Case for Affirmative Action* (Ithaca, N.Y.: Cornell University Press, 1991), 89.

10. Wise, 2.

11. Kathleen Parker, *Executive Edge* (Emmaus, Pa.: National Center for Career Strategies, 1990).

12. For further discussion, see Ezorsky, 44.

13. Thanks to Patti Wolter for her article, "Is Racism at Work Where You Work?" *SALT* (September 1992): 6-11, for many of the ideas in this section.

14. Ibid., 9.

Chapter Eleven

1. Tom Skinner, "Undoing Racism: Coming Together in Our Cit-

ies," *Urban Connections: Inter Mennonite Urban Newsletter* 7 (Summer 1991): 1.

2. Roberto Chene, excerpted from mimeograph "Improving Cross-Cultural Relationships: Being Allies for Each Other" (Albuquerque: Southwest Institute for Cross-Cultural Relationships).

3. Elizabeth Martinez and Louis Head, "Media White-Out of Environmental Racism," *IFCO News* (Fall 1992): 8.

4. Ibid., 8.

5. Ibid.

6. Horace Seldon, "Working Against Racism: What Needs to Be Changed?" in *Convictions About Racism in the United States of America: Essays and Articles by Horace Seldon* (Boston: Community Change, Inc., 1992), 8.

7. Louise Derman-Sparks, María Gutiérrez, and Carol B. Phillips, *Teaching Young Children to Resist Bias: What Parents Can Do* (Washington, D.C.: National Association for the Education of Young Children), unnumbered pamphlet.

8. Herbert Kohl, "The Politics of Children's Literature: The Story of Rosa Parks and the Montgomery Bus Boycott," *Rethinking Schools* (January/February 1991): 11-13.

9. *Creating a New Community: God's People Overcoming Racism,* Leader's Guide Eleanor A. Moore, ed. (Nashville: Graded Press, 1989), 51. Written by Shalom Education, an Ecumenical Peace Education Organization, Chicago, Ill. Copyright © 1989 by Graded Press. Reprinted with permission.

10. I was eventually hired for another position, so I cannot say I bore that cost too long.

Appendix A

1. The birthday of Martin Luther King, Jr. (1929-1968), a civil rights and nonviolence leader, is celebrated as a national holiday in the United States on January 15. Various states' commemorations are held on other days in January.

2. The Acadians were French settlers in what is now Nova Scotia. In 1755, they were rounded up by the British and expelled. Many fled to what was then French Louisiana, where their descendants today are known as Cajuns. Other sizable numbers returned to the Madawaska region of Maine and New Brunswick. Henry Wadsworth Longfellow's poem "Evangeline" depicts this episode (which the United Nations would now label as genocide).

3. Louis Riel (1844-1885) was a métis (mixed native and French)

leader from Assiniboia, Manitoba. The Riel Rebellions of 1869 and 1884-1885 established short-lived provisional governments which attempted to resist English domination in settlement of the Canadian West. Riel was tried and hanged in Regina on November 16, 1885. He is regarded by many as a French-Canadian and Native people's patriot.

Resource List

Introduction

One of the goals I have in writing this book is to provide the resources necessary for evaluating the effects of white privilege. The main ideas we have looked at so far have laid a good foundation for meeting that goal. Chapters on prejudice, racism, white privilege, affirmative action, and the effects of racism have been designed to help the reader understand white privilege and begin the healing process.

However, we need to draw from as many resources as possible to further our movement toward the river. And so I have included an extensive listing of resources available for further education. While not a complete list, the resources provide a sample of what is currently available in this field. The suggested books, articles, videos, study guides, curricula, and workshops that follow represent a variety of approaches. Many approaches are similar to ideas found in this book. Some are different. A few of the resources are more appropriate for people who have only begun to consider racism. Others will be more helpful for those who have spent extended time on this subject.

I am not intimately familiar with every resource, but I have included comments whenever possible as an aid in discerning which resources best meet individual needs.

If you are reading this book in a group setting, whether Sunday school, study group, or house church, I encourage you to take time to engage in some strategic planning for your next steps before spending time with the resource list. Once you know your objectives, you will make better use of the resources. For example, if your immediate goal is to build relationships with sister churches, you will look for different resources than if you decide to hold a workshop on white privilege.

Ten suggestions for talking about racism

Before moving to the list of resources, let me share a list of ten elements that I think essential for encouraging movement toward the healing river. The ideas are not new, but they act as a concise reminder of the main ideas found elsewhere in this book.

1. Build on an analysis of power and privilege. Prejudice reduction and cross-cultural training seminars provide essential tools for equipping people to function in an increasingly diverse church. These training formats need to be connected to a discussion of white privilege and systemic racism. Without that analysis, we train people who are aware of their prejudice and able to cross cultures, but unable to understand their role in perpetuating systemic racism.

2. Work to continually tie together action and reflection. European-American church groups sometimes have a tendency to analyze an issue to the point of inaction. Working with church groups from other ethnic backgrounds, practicing how to respond to racial jokes, or working to stop police brutality toward people of color are just a few examples of how to connect action with reflection. In this way, the process itself serves as a model of the outcome desired.

3. Create a safe place for healthy expression of emotion. Whether in a weekend seminar or a fifteen-minute conversation, the topic of racism comes prepackaged with emotion. Directed storytelling in small group settings allows sharing of common hopes and hurts. Guilt, fear, and anger are among the most common emotions expressed in discussion of racism.

4. Reserve time for cultural sharing and discovery. Even in supposedly monocultural environments, great diversity exists among individual family histories, customs, and traditions. When we understand the strengths and weaknesses of our culture, we are better equipped to appreciate and work with other cultures. By differentiating our cultural heritage from that of the dominant norm, we expose the shallowness of shopping malls, fast-food restaurants, pop icons, and movie stars.

5. Discourage discussion that leads to a classification of good and bad people. As with any evil that takes on systemic proportions, individual attitudes and actions may not be the final determiner of who is at fault for racism. For example, many people of European descent are not aware of the tremendous privilege they receive simply by having white skin. They are not bad people because they are unaware of this. Once aware of white privilege, we need to hold each other accountable for what we do with that awareness. In this way, we refuse to judge who is good or bad.

6. Encourage study of history. As time and interest allow, there are many resources available to help people reevaluate the version of history they have been taught. Whether one was told "The people watched the slaves pick cotton" or "The African-American people, forced to pick cotton, watched the white people standing by," influences current response to issues of welfare, health care, or unemployment. Be aware of authors' backgrounds and perspectives, whether in elementary text books or today's newspapers, as a first step toward critical thinking.

7. Show how racism injures everyone. Racism has too long been portrayed as a problem people of color have to solve by themselves, for themselves. In North America, racism is a white problem that damages everyone. That harm does not take the same form among people of European descent as it does in racial ethnic communities, but the damage is no less serious. Racism creates false assumptions of worth; encourages fear between racial groups; disrupts church harmony; builds up the myth of whiteness.

8. Be gentle, but uncompromising. During a recent discussion of racism in an all-white private high school, one student insisted that most people on welfare were "black and lazy." The presenter had been trying to build up student awareness of the strengths of their own culture but had to stop and state that the majority of people on welfare are white, not people of color. A thousand myths layer popular consciousness about race and culture. We need to be sure not to inadvertently perpetuate them ourselves. And so part of our homework as white people is to read the books and other resources that provide a more factual representation of history and contemporary issues.

9. Ground your discussion in Scripture. Christ's example of crossing cultural barriers, Luke's account of early church struggles over Gentile inclusion, and Paul's admonitions to build up the community of Christ provide important scriptural background. Examination of the many cultural contributions (Hellenic, Hebraic, Greek, Roman, Egyptian, European, Latino) to the formation and growth of the Christian church may also be helpful. In a similar vein, study of how the church has portrayed Christ in paintings and pictures can be uncomfortable, but revealing (Did Christ really have white skin and blue eyes?).

10. Resist attempts at colorblind education. People who say, "I see a person—not white, black, red, or brown," may be well meaning but ignore a large part of humanity. God gave us a wonderful diversity that needs to be celebrated, recognized, and built up. When we aim for a colorblind stance, we merely demean cultures differing from the dominant norm. In North America, people of European descent hold the majority of power and therefore have determined "appropriate" cultural expression. As we in the church learn from our many cultural expressions, share power as equals, and work together to spread the good news, we need to be ever more aware of color, culture, and ethnicity. A colorblind person cannot appreciate the many hues of God's creation.

Books/Articles
Theory/Reflection

Allport, Gordon W. *The Nature of Prejudice*. Reading, Mass.: Addison-Wesley Publishing Company, 1986. Pioneering work on prejudice.

Barndt, Joseph. *Dismantling Racism: The Continuing Challenge to White America*. Minneapolis, Minn.: Augsburg Fortress, 1991. Extensive explication of racism with a strong call for movement to action and change. A "must read" for European-Americans.

Bell, Derrick. *Faces at the Bottom of the Well: The Permanence of Racism*. New York: Basic Books, 1992. Through a series of short stories and accompanying fictional "conversations," Bell proposes that racism is fundamentally woven through the fabric of the U.S. Calls for new methods of working against racism that move beyond strategies of the civil rights era.

Bowser, Benjamin P., and Raymond Hunt, eds. *Impacts of Racism on White Americans*. Newbury Park, Calif.: Sage Publications, 1981. A collection of essays on negative impacts of racism on European-Americans. Many of the essays are written from a psychological perspective.

Brown, Hubert L. *Black and Mennonite: A Search for Identity*. Scottdale, Pa.: Herald Press, 1976. Essential reading for gaining an understanding of what it means for someone to enter into the Mennonite Church from a culture other than European-American.

Carter, Stephen L. *Reflections of an Affirmative Action Baby*. New York: Basic Books, 1991. Writes from his perspective as an African-American academic. Makes a case for openness of dialogue on affirmative action that refrains from labeling different perspectives.

Cobbs, Price M., and William A. Grier. *Black Rage*. New York: Basic Books, 1968. Two African-American psychologists explore the inner conflicts and desperation of black men's life in America. Story-based and easy to read.

Elizondo, Virgilio. *Galilean Journey: The Mexican-American Promise*. Maryknoll, New York: Orbis Books, 1983. Portrays the cultural context of Jesus of Nazareth in Palestine and notes parallels with Mexican-Americans in North America.

Felder, Cain Hope. "Out of Africa I Have Called My Son," *The Other Side* 28 (November-December 1992): 8-14. Examines the cultural and "racial" background of Jesus of Nazareth and other biblical figures.

Green, Stanley W. "How Do We Get Rid of Racism in the Mennonite Church?" *Gospel Herald* 85 (February 11, 1992): 5-7. Contains important suggestions for the Mennonite Church.

Hacker, Andrew. "The Myths of Racial Division," *The New Republic* (March 23, 1992): 21-25. Presents contemporary demographical portrait of changing nature of race.

Hooks, Bell. *Ain't I a Woman?: Black Women and Feminism*. Boston: South End Press, 1982. Explores dynamics of race and gender in the American context.

Hooks, Bell. "Reworking History," *The Other Side* 29 (March-April 1993): 20-26. Forthright examination of whiteness.

Knowles, Louis L., and Kenneth Prewitt. *Institutional Racism in America*. Englewood Cliffs, N.J.: Prentice-Hall, 1969. Although dated, outlines extent of institutional racism in a framework still applicable today.

Lamar, Jake. "The Trouble with You People: A Black Journalist Ponders the Crisis of White America," *Utne Reader* 51 (May/June 1992): 82-87. Refreshing reversal of who usually writes about whom.

Martin, Ann. "Bringing Racism to Center Stage," *Gospel Herald* 84 (Nov. 5, 1991): 1-3. Draws from racial ethnic leaders of the Mennonite Church.

McIntosh, Peggy. "White Privilege: Unpacking the Invisible Knapsack," *Peace and Freedom* (July/August 1989): 10-12. Seminal work on understanding white privilege.

Moore, Robert B. *Racism in the English Language*. New York: Council on Interracial Books for Children, 1976. Extensive examination of the many ways racism is perpetuated through often unintentional use of language.

Nelson-Pallmeyer, Jack. *War Against the Poor: Low-Intensity Conflict and Christian Faith*. Maryknoll, N.Y.: Orbis Books, 1989. Forceful examination of the practice of low-intensity conflict in North America and two-thirds world settings. Lays bare some of the systems undergirding racism.

Schlabach, Gerald W. *And Who Is My Neighbor?: Poverty, Privilege, and the Gospel of Christ*. Scottdale, Pa.: Herald Press, 1990. Provides easily accessible introduction to solidarity with the poor and oppressed. Thoroughly grounded in Scripture and designed for small-group study.

Schwartz, Barry N., and Robert Disch. *White Racism: It's History, Pathology and Practice*. New York: Dell Publishing Co., 1970. Brings together an impressive collection of essays on whites as the source of racism. Includes essays by William Stringfellow, Robert Coles, and others.

Seldon, Horace. *Convictions About Racism in the United States of America*. Boston: Community Change, Inc., 1992. A wide-ranging collection of three dozen essays on racism by Community Change, Inc., executive director, Horace Seldon. Written by a European-American for primarily European-American audiences.

Skinner, Tom. "Undoing Racism: Coming Together in Our Cities," *Urban Connections* 7 (Summer 1991): 1-2. This entire edition of *Urban Connections* contains many helpful essays written by Mennonites working to dismantle racism.

Terry, Robert W. *For Whites Only*. Grand Rapids, Mich.: William B. Eerdmans Publishing Co., 1970. Grapples with what it means to be white in a multiethnic world.

Yette, Samuel F. *The Choice: The Issue of Black Survival in America.* New York: Berkeley Publishing Corporation, 1971. Some statistics may be dated but still serves to trace the machinations of racism through politics and public policy.

Application

Bond, Julian. "Civil Rights in the Popular Culture," *Southern Changes* 14 (Spring 1992): 1-7. Examines popular portrayal of the civil rights movement.

Cobbler, Michael L. *Cross-Cultural Evangelism: Helping Congregations Reach Out.* Minneapolis, Minn.: Augsburg Fortress, 1991. Helps congregations engage in evangelism.

Ezorsky, Gertrude. *Racism and Justice: The Case for Affirmative Action.* Ithaca, N.Y.: Cornell University Press, 1991. A well-documented case for the success of affirmative action. Short and easy to read.

Kochman, Thomas. *Black and White Styles in Conflict.* Chicago: University of Chicago Press, 1981. Classic work on the differences in dealing with conflict between African-Americans and European-Americans.

McGinnis, Kathleen and James *Parenting for Peace and Justice.* Maryknoll, N.Y.: Orbis Books, 1981. Includes a chapter on encouraging involvement with other cultures. Based on authors' own experiences with their children.

Rice, Chris. "From Caseworkers to Comrades: The Role of Whites in the Black Community," *Urban Connections* (October 1989): 8-11. Important reading for any European-American working in African-American environments.

Stoner, John K. *Called to Be Peacemakers: A New Call to Peacemaking Workbook.* Akron, Pa.: New Call to Peacemaking, 1992. Contains eight-page chapter on peacemaking between races and cultures with clear analysis and concrete action suggestions.

Wise, Tim. "Affirmative Action and the Politics of White Resentment." *Blueprint for Social Justice* 45 (October 1991): 1-7. Includes extensive documentation and logical argument for affirmative action.

History

Barrett, Lois. *The Vision and the Reality: The Story of Home Missions in the General Conference Mennonite Church.* Newton, Kan.: Faith & Life Press, 1983. Deals specifically with church work in the domestic setting. Extensive examination of work among Native Americans.

Bechler, Le Roy. *The Black Mennonite Church in North America, 1886-1986.* Scottdale, Pa.: Herald Press, 1986. Good summary of the beginnings of the African-American church in North America. Contains extensive statistical analysis of African-American membership in the Mennonite Church through 1980 (written by a European-American).

Brown, Dee. *Bury My Heart at Wounded Knee: An Indian History of the American West.* New York: Holt, Rinehart and Winston, 1971. Gives historical insight into struggle of Native Americans not found in many other texts.

Falcón, Rafael. *The Hispanic Mennonite Church in North America, 1932-1982.* Scottdale, Pa.: Herald Press, 1986. Extensive documentation of the background, beginnings, organization, and charter congregations of the Hispanic Mennonite Church in North America.

Harding, Vincent. *There Is a River: The Black Struggle for Freedom in America.* Harcourt Brace Jovanovich, 1981. Reprinted New York: Vintage Books, 1983. Meticulously documents history of African-Americans in North America. Places often ignored historical figures in the context of their struggle for freedom.

MacMaster, Richard K. *Land, Piety, Peoplehood : The Establishment of Mennonite Communities in America, 1683-1790.* Vol. 1 of *The Mennonite Experience in America.* Scottdale, Pa.: Herald Press, 1985. Contains references to early Mennonite response to Native Americans and African-Americans.

Schlabach, Theron. *Peace, Faith, Nation: Mennonites and Amish in Nineteenth Century America.* Vol. 2 of *The Mennonite Experience in America.* Scottdale, Pa.: Herald Press, 1988. Contains more references to early Mennonite response to Native Americans and African-Americans.

Takaki, R. *Strangers from a Different Shore: A History of Asian Americans.* Boston: Little Brown and Co., 1989. Tells a solid history of Asian-Americans.

Weatherford, Jack. *Indian Givers: How the Indians of the Americas Transformed the World.* New York: Ballantine Books, 1988. A profoundly disturbing yet intriguing examination of the immense body of learning and resource Native Americans have brought to the world.

Education

Clemens, Sydney Gurewitz. "A Dr. Martin Luther King, Jr. Curriculum: Playing the Dream," *Young Children* (January 1988): 6-11, 59-62. Presents concrete suggestions for working with young children to experience King's dream.

Derman-Sparks, Louise. *Anti-Bias Curriculum: Tools for Empowering Young Children.* Washington, D.C.: National Association for Education of Young Children, 1989. Describes developmental tasks, goals, and activities for fostering children's healthy identity and attitudes about race, ethnicity, gender, and disabilities and how teachers can work with parents.

Derman-Sparks, Louise, María Gutiérrez, and Carol B. Phillips. "Teaching Young Children to Resist Bias: What Parents Can Do," National Association for the Education of Young Children, unnumbered pamphlet. Excellent, concise resource for parents.

Hampson, Tom, and Loretta Whalen. *Tales of the Heart: Affective Approaches to Global Education.* New York: Friendship Press, 1991. Contains excellent section on enemy-making and prejudice.

Katz, Judith. *White Awareness: Handbook for Anti-Racism Training.* Norman, Okla.: University of Oklahoma Press, 1978. In addition to many examples of group exercises for understanding racism, the book provides an analytical framework based on the understanding that racism is a white problem to be solved by white people.

Kohl, Herbert. "The Politics of Children's Literature: The Story of Rosa Parks and the Montgomery Bus Boycott," *Rethinking Schools* (January/February 1991): 10-13. Insightful essay on how children's literature can be presented in a way that encourages social change.

Kozol, Jonathan. *Savage Inequalities: Children in America's Schools.* New York: Crown Publishers, 1991. A controversial, uncompromising book that provides a searing look into the inequities of the U.S. public education system. Highlights differences in funding along racial lines.

Phillips, Carol Brunson. "Nurturing Diversity for Today's Children and Tomorrow's Leaders," *Young Children* (January 1988): 42-47. Excellent article for educators of young children.

Criminal justice

Currie, Elliott. *Confronting Crime: An American Challenge.* New York: Pantheon Books, 1985. Defies any attempt to label as conservative or liberal. Sharp analysis of racial ethnic dynamics of crime.

Ogawa, Brian. *Color of Justice: Culturally Sensitive Treatment of Minority Crime Victims.* Sacramento: Office of the Governor, State of California, 1990. Presents racism as one of many problems facing racial ethnics in the criminal justice system. Chapter five engages directly with issues of racism and color blindness associated with power and privilege.

Zehr, Howard. *Changing Lenses: A New Focus for Crime and Justice.* Scottdale, Pa.: Herald Press, 1990. Takes a look at the criminal justice system and provides a new way of seeking justice that breaks out of current patterns crippled by racism.

Worship aids

"Racism: No Room at the Table." Bread for the World. Gives creative ideas on celebrating diversity in a worship setting. Write to BFW, 802 Rhode Island Ave., NE, Washington, DC 20018.

Curriculum/Study guides

Anti-Defamation League of B'nai B'rith. *Being Fair and Being Free.* A set of twenty activities for high school students dealing with the nature of prejudice and the impact of prejudice on individuals and nations. Available from Anti-Defamation League of B'nai B'rith, 823 United Nations Plaza, New York, NY 10017; (212) 490-2525.

Bullard, Sara, ed. "Teaching Tolerance." Montgomery, Ala.: Southern Poverty Law Center, 1991. Excellent resource for educators desiring to welcome differences and delight in sharing across cultures. Available from Teaching Tolerance, 400 Washington Ave., Montgomery, AL 36104.

Commission, Office of the Human Relations. *Human Relations Training Manual*. Rockville, Md.: Montgomery County Government, 1988. Concrete training examples for use in workplace settings. Contains exercises on prejudice, white awareness, cross-cultural communication. Available from Office of the Human Relations Commission, 164 Rollins Avenue, Rockville, MD 20852-4067; (301) 468-4260.

Ho, Liang. *Cross-Cultural Swinging: A Handbook for Self-Awareness and Multi-Cultural Living!* Honolulu, Hawaii: Liang Ho, 1990. Takes anthropological approach to understanding culture. Contains charts and exercises. Available from Cross-Cultural Manual, 2238 Kaala Way, Honolulu, HI 96822; (808) 941-8626.

LaRoque, Emma, ed. *In Search of Peace: A Challenge from Four Non-White North American Mennonites*. Akron, Pa.: Mennonite Central Committee U.S. Peace Section, 1976. Dated but still powerful in basic critique.

Matthias, Dody S. *Working for Life: Dismantling Racism*. Lima, Ohio: Fairway Press, 1990. An excellent study guide that moves from definitions of racism through examination of racism in the church to setting up support structures for the long haul. Available from The CSS Publishing Company, 628 South Main St., Lima, Ohio, 45804; 1 (800) 328-4648 or (419) 229-2665.

Matthias, Dody S. *Racism: from Guilt to Grace*. Minneapolis, Minn.: Augsburg Fortress, 1991. Tightly constructed study guide for adult study groups and other small, short-term settings. Provides four small-group study sessions based in the Lutheran tradition but easily applied to other faith traditions. Available from Augsburg Fortress, 426 S. 5th St., Minneapolis, MN 55415-1434; (612) 330-3300.

Mennonite Board of Missions. "How Tolerant Are You?" *Global Christians* 57-64. Brings together articles providing insights on Asians, Hispanics, Native Americans, Africans, Jews, Arabs, and Russians. Number 57 includes "tolerance quiz." Available from Mennonite

Board of Missions, P.O. Box 370, Elkhart, IN 46515-0370; (219) 294-7523.

Mennonite Conciliation Service. "Responding to Prejudice," *Conciliation Quarterly Newsletter* 9 (Spring 1990); "Undoing Racism in our Institutions," *Conciliation Quarterly Newsletter* 11 (Spring 1992). Although not set up for a study format per se, both issues include insightful articles on the nature of prejudice and bringing an end to institutional racism. Available from Mennonite Conciliation Service, MCC US, 21 S. 12th St., P.O. Box 500, Akron, PA 17501-0500; (717) 859-3889.

Moore, Eleanor A., ed. *Creating a New Community: God's People Overcoming Racism*. Nashville, Tenn.: Graded Press, 1989. Best suited for those looking for an extensive process (twelve sessions) that leads toward community action. Written for Christian audiences and includes small-group exercises, journaling suggestions, worship ideas, and action examples. Available from Shalom Education, 1448 East 53rd St., Chicago, IL 60615; (312) 363-2020.

Verchot, Michael, and Jim Wallis, eds. "America's Original Sin: A Study Guide on White Racism." Expanded edition. Washington, D.C.: Sojourners, 1992. Brings together extensive series of articles on racism and related issues. Set up for congregational discussion groups. Available from Sojourners Resource Center, 2401 15th St., NW, Washington, DC 20009; (202) 328-8842.

Womack, Paula, and Ken Sehested. "Domestic Sister Churches: Pairing Congregations of Different Racial/Ethnic Backgrounds." Special issue of *PeaceWork*. Memphis: Baptist Peace Fellowship of North America, 1990. Contains many articles about churches that have come together across cultures as well as concrete suggestions for congregations considering seeking out sister churches. Available from Baptist Peace Fellowship of North America, 499 Patterson St., Memphis, TN 38111; (901) 324-7675.

Videos

A Class Divided. Anti-Defamation League of B'nai B'rith. A blue-eye/brown-eye experiment conducted with third-graders in 1970 is reviewed by those students as adults in 1984. Shows the same experiment conducted at a prison with 175 employees. Available from Anti-Defamation League of B'nai B'rith, 823 United Nations Plaza, New York, NY 10017; (212) 490-2525.

A Time for Justice: America's Civil Rights Movement. Montgomery: Southern Poverty Law Center, 1992. Excellent resource for educators. Comes with detailed lesson plans and supplementary publication. Available from Civil Rights Kit, Teaching Tolerance, 400 Washington Ave., Montgomery, AL 36104.

Anti-Bias Curriculum. Louise Derman-Sparks and Bert Atkinson. Shows four teachers working with children, ages 2-5, in various early childhood settings and discusses steps for implementing anti-bias curriculum. Discussion guide included. Available from National Association for the Education of Young Children, 1509 16th St., NW, Washington, DC 20036-1426; 1 (800) 424-2460.

"Beyond the News: Racism." Harrisonburg, Va.: Mennonite Media Ministries, 1992. Pastors and church leaders, a lawyer and an author examine prejudice, racism and white privilege and how they affect jobs, education, the judicial system, and the church. Study guide included. Available from Mennonite Media Ministries, 1251 Virginia Ave., Harrisonburg, VA 22801-2497; 1 (800) 999-3534 or (703) 434-6701.

Eyes on the Prize: America's Civil Rights Years 1954-1965. Boston: Blackside, Inc., 1987. Insightful, comprehensive, and moving history of the civil rights movement.

Face to Face: Seeking Racial Reconciliation. 2100 Productions. Madison, Wis.: Inter-Varsity Christian Fellowship of the USA, 1990. Emphasizes the importance of dealing with racial conflicts, intentionally building relationships across racial lines, and of worshiping in multicultural environments; examines policies, social norms, organizational structures, tokenism, and power as undergirding forces beneath racism. Available from 2100 Productions, P.O. Box 7895, Madison, WI 53707-7895; 1 (800) 828-2100 or (608) 274-9001.

"L.A.: Voices from the Ashes." Harrisonburg, Va.: Mennonite Media Ministries, 1992. Shows inside reality of Los Angeles riots from the perspective of church leaders and the hope that rises from the ashes of destruction. Comes with helpful study guides. Available from

Mennonite Media Ministries, 1251 Virginia Ave., Harrisonburg, VA 22801-2497; 1 (800) 999-3534 or (703) 434-6701.

"Racism 101." Explores why racism and bigotry persist on college campuses. A PBS award-winner for senior high and adults. Available from Anti-Defamation League of B'nai B'rith, 823 United Nations Plaza, New York, NY 10017; (212) 490-2525.

Groups

COMMUNITAS
method— multiracial training team for workshops and consulting on racism and prejudice reduction.
contact— Andrea Ayvazian and Beverly Tatum, 245 Main St., #207, N. Hampton, MA 01060; (413) 586-3088.

Community Change, Inc.
method— present workshops, do consultations and audits, teach courses, produce publications, maintain a resource library, develop a drama group, and prepare civil rights internships (over twenty years experience in all the above).
contact— Horace Seldon, executive director, Community Change, Inc., 14 Beacon St., Room 702, Boston, MA 02108; (617) 523-0555.

CRC Publications—Cross-Cultural Workshops
method— this publishing body of the Christian Reformed Church provides self-contained workshop packages of 5-10 sessions for use in small or large groups; includes leader's guide, handouts integrated with Scripture, and group activities; packets available on confronting discrimination, reducing bias in children, and working across cultures.
contact— Gary Teja, curriculum editor for cross-cultural materials, CRC Publications, 2850 Kalamazoo Ave., SE, Grand Rapids, MI 49560; (616) 246-0825.

DISMANTLING RACISM PROJECT
method— workshops dealing with personal and institutional manifestations of racism, particularly for white audiences.
contact— Mary Webber, The National Conference of Christians and Jews, 721 Olive, Suite 915, St. Louis, MO 63101.

EXCHANGE PROJECT OF THE PEACE DEVELOPMENT FUND
method—provide workshops on dismantling racism; also have video
available on the experience of two men, one white and one
black, looking for jobs, apartments, etc.
contact—Elizabeth Rankin, The Exchange Project, P.O. Box 270, Amherst, MA 01004; (413) 256-8306.

MENNONITE CHURCH OFFICES: "DEVELOPING HARMONY
THROUGH DIVERSITY"
analysis—begin with understanding cultural differences according to
basic values held by different racial ethnic groups; use perception exercises; some church structural analysis; scriptural reflection; principles for developing multicultural relationships; excellent presentation on cultural bias and resulting gaps in resources.
method—small group work; perception exercises; theoretical constructs; group discussion.
contact—Brent Foster, Carlos Romero, Noel Santiago, Box 1245, Elkhart, IN 46515; (219) 294-7523.

NATIONAL COALITION BUILDING INSTITUTE
analysis—guilt is the glue that holds prejudice in place; everyone has
been a victim of prejudice; sharing common experiences of
pain and joy can bring about coalitions across ethnic and
racial lines; includes elements of conflict resolution/mediation training; importance of sharing different
perspectives and history of peoples.
method—prejudice reduction workshops center on exploring pain of
past experiences; presence of humor; sharing fears and associations with different stereotypes; centers on training
trainers for purposes of building coalitions.
contact—National Coalition Building Institute, 1835 K St., NW, Suite
715, Washington, DC 20006; (202) 785-9400; FAX (202)
785-3385.
—Mennonite-related multiracial training team of Nancy Sider and Gerald Hudson may be contacted at 251 Park Place,
Harrisonburg, VA 22801; (703) 433-9879.

PEOPLE'S INSTITUTE FOR SURVIVAL AND BEYOND
analysis—long-time community organizers present excellent analysis of poor communities and definition of racism; emphasis
on culture, history, and understanding systems; promotes

values and vision for work in poor communities; one of the most worthwhile and challenging workshops available.

method—weekend workshops with both people of color and members of dominant culture; create safe zone for exploring racism; sharing of cultures; emphasis on lecture and discussion; some small-group activities.

contact—People's Institute for Survival and Beyond, 1444 N. Johnson St., New Orleans, LA 70116; (504) 944-2354.

SOUTHWEST CENTER FOR CROSS-CULTURAL RELATIONSHIPS

analysis—cultural diversity is enriching to all, equality between cultural groups should be the prime characteristic which guides cross-cultural interactions; based in field of mental health; emphasizes appropriate behavior of allies; recognizes need to reconcile personal and structural diversity by establishing and maintaining peer relationships across cultural and racial lines.

method—weekend workshops and written materials foster a sense of community and common purpose among those concerned about cross-cultural interaction; includes emphases on counseling and mediation skills in multicultural social settings.

contact—Roberto Chene, 1112 Calle del Ranchero, NE, Albuquerque, NM 87106; (505) 262-0264.

SYNAPSES

analysis—defines racism as prejudice plus the power to enforce it, a white privileged position; asks European-Americans to recognize white skin privilege, confess that white privilege keeps our power intact and helps keep us comfortable, repent of our willful ignorance; importance of seeing white culture and history as one among many; a long-term process.

method—varying length workshops depending upon who is organizing them; working as equals helps promote understanding of other cultures.

contact—Synapses, 1821 W. Cullerton, Chicago, IL 60608; (312) 421-5513.

VISIONS, INC.

analysis—combines examination of personal prejudices, institutional racism, and effects of racism with strategies for changing dysfunctional intraracial and interracial behavior.

method—four-day workshops on multi-culturalism that integrate Transactional Analysis/Gestalt theory and techniques with other personal and community change models.

contact—VISIONS, Inc. 68 Park Ave., Cambridge, MA 02138; (617) 876-9257.

Additional resource listings

Anti-Defamation League of B'nai B'rith, 823 United Nations Plaza, New York, NY 10017; (212) 490-2525.

Bilingual Publications (materials in Spanish), 270 Lafayette St., New York, NY 10012; (212) 431-3500; FAX (212) 431-3567.

Global Village Toys, 2210 Wilshire Blvd., Suite 262, Santa Monica, CA 90403.

Multicultural Resources Center, 1205 Palmyra Ave., Richmond, VA 23227.

Syracuse Cultural Workers, Box 6367, Syracuse, NY 13217; (315) 474-1132.

Scripture Index

Subject Index

V
Virginia, Richmond, 75

W
Walker, Carmen, 60
Walton, Robin, 159-161
Wangerin, Walter, Jr., 98
Washington, George, 99, 108
Washington, Michael, 105
Whigham, Ertell, 27

White
    history of, 105-106
    skin privilege, 107-113
Willems, Dirk, 123
William, Daniel Hale, 78
Winterbourne Elementary
    School, 47
Wise, Tim, 144
Wright, Jane C., 78

Z
Zinn, Howard, 99
Zuercher, Melanie, 161-162

The Author

FROM 1987 to 1993, Jody Miller Shearer lived and worked in New Orleans. He was program coordinator of Mennonite Central Committee's (MCC) work in that city, administrator of a program from families of homicide victims, and editor of a social justice magazine, *Blueprint for Social Justice*. For two years he also edited the Gulf States Mennonite Conference newsletter, *The Fellowship*.

Jody has written extensively and in a variety of publications on topics of racism and white privilege. He is currently MCC U.S. Peace and Justice Ministries staff associate for racism awareness.

Jody is married to Cheryl Miller Shearer. He met Cheryl while studying English at Eastern Mennonite College in Harrisonburg, Virginia, the same town in which he was born. Cheryl and Jody have two sons, Dylan (1990) and Zachary (1992).

The Shearers live in Lancaster (Pa.) and attend East Chestnut Mennonite Church.